MW01628659

SAN FRANCISCO BY SEASON

Recipes to savor from the
San Francisco Chronicle

CONTENTS

FALL

WINTER

FOREWORD

CHRISTIAN REYNOSO, *Bounty columnist for San Francisco Chronicle*

When I started writing for the San Francisco Chronicle food section in February 2020, it never occurred to me that one day I might write a foreword for a cookbook, let alone this cookbook, just a handful of years later. The San Francisco Chronicle is the Big City Newspaper I remember being in those coin-op newsstands that I grew up seeing on the streets of Sonoma. There was actually one outside my parents' restaurant near the town square. As a kid, I would peer in, wondering why newspapers were so important that they, out of everything, were the only things sold in bins on the sidewalk. Years later I'd learn that journalism was quite important, that the Chronicle was the region's premier news source, and that pieces of paper with words on them, and sometimes pictures, can matter. I'm a bit biased, but I think the food section, and especially its cooking and recipe articles, is probably the most important section at the Chron.

It's a digital world now and I read the Chronicle on the app, but pieces of paper with words on them are still important, especially cookbooks. Why? Well, besides the whole tangible, being-able-to-turn-beautiful-pages thing, this cookbook is full of recipes that can be your collection, your chronicle, of a time and a place — and that place is the robust home cooking culture of San Francisco and the greater Bay Area.

My food origin story began back in my parents' restaurant, but it was 2011 when I realized I didn't know how to cook with different kinds of extra-virgin olive oil properly and that there were more than a couple of vinegars in existence. So I got a job as a line cook at a wine bar, hoping to learn. Then, in 2015, I started working at the San Francisco institution of California cookery, Zuni Cafe. I stayed for five years, and part of the reason was the daily changing menu. Every day, like in school, we'd learn how to prepare, pair and enjoy produce in new ways. I learned every station and became sous chef. Eventually, I wrote lunch and dinner menus, applying what I learned from my mentors, adding my own style when it made sense.

Writing those menus, trying out a new dish here and there, was a lot like recipe development. I learned to love culinary tinkering. Critically thinking about how to create a dish that not only I loved, but one that guests would order, became one of my favorite parts of my job. I started taking all the journalism classes I could and assisted local food writers, like Jessica Battilana. And I began writing about food and developing my own recipes.

A month after I started writing my column for the Chronicle, the world changed dramatically. The pandemic shut down almost everything. Only the hardcore loyalists were going to the farmers' market. Several Saturday mornings at the Ferry Plaza market, it seemed like someone saved me a parking spot in front, so I could walk over and shop till I dropped in what seemed like my very own market.

Pantry staple cookery was everyone's focus. All of a sudden, it felt like asking folks to go outside to get kumquats was maybe dangerous? Nevertheless, I learned that the aspiring home cook was alive and thriving during this time.

Besides actual cooking, it also gave people time to think more about where the heck our food comes from, which cuisines they loved cooking and the historical background of dishes. People slowed down. They were tasting and seasoning their food. They were also watching cooking videos and learning to love, or at least like, this very human thing a bit more: cooking and eating.

Friends of mine who would normally cringe at posting a food photo would upload pics of their proud culinary creations, whether it was thoughtful, elaborate or silly. And we certainly can't forget about how a bubbling sourdough starter became, for some, a new roommate. Acquaintances would reach out and ask me for advice about this or that. It was an energizing time to be a newbie in the recipe-writing world, and despite the tumult, my recipe column brought me solace and purpose.

This book is full of beautiful recipes. As I said, some are mine, like my buttery and very garlicky Garlic Noodles With Summer Squash & Parmesan (see page 65), an ode to the Vietnamese American dish born in San Francisco, or a recipe for BLT Tostadas (see page 67), which I wrote while on a sabbatical in Mexico City. A lot of my recipes are great platforms for you to adopt and make your own, too. For the noodles recipe in particular, you could easily swap out halved cherry tomatoes or snap peas for the squash. For the tostada, it might be harder to change much and have it still be a BLT, but I'd encourage you to use crunchy tortillas as a base for all kinds toppings, from an herbaceous chicken salad to a smashed avocado spiked with lime juice, sauteed spring vegetables and a crumble of feta. However you cook out of this book, I hope you enjoy it.

Pieces of paper with words on them are still important, especially cookbooks. Why? Well, besides the whole tangible, being-able-to-turn-beautiful-pages thing, this cookbook is full of recipes that can be your collection, your chronicle, of a time and a place — and that place is the robust home cooking culture of San Francisco and the greater Bay Area.

INTRODUCTION

JANELLE BITKER, *San Francisco Chronicle Food & Wine senior editor*

In the San Francisco Bay Area, we have high standards when it comes to food. We spend our nights out huddled over delicate handmade pastas, cheesy tacos, crunchy Burmese salads and garlicky Dungeness crab with even more garlicky noodles. At home, we want big, restaurant-worthy flavor. We want it without too much fuss. And we want to use local, seasonal ingredients, because we know they taste better.

On the San Francisco Chronicle Food & Wine team, we are obsessed with food. We have been for decades. It's our duty to steer readers toward noteworthy meals, to reflect our region's fierce passion for all things edible. Amid ups and downs, the Bay Area remains a thrilling place to eat, a hotbed of innovation, national attention and plentiful local produce. Home to crucial American culinary history, it's a place where classic restaurants are revered alongside modern fine dining destinations.

The last San Francisco Chronicle cookbook came out in 2001 — a royal blue textbook, equipped with 375 recipes and zero photos. Our history of recipe contributors is epic: Flo Braker, Georgeanne Brennan, Janet Fletcher, Jacqueline Higuera McMahan, Marlena Spieler and Joanne Weir are just some of the regulars who have graced our pages. Much has changed since 2001. The internet upended the way we eat, cook and consume news. We publish fewer recipes now, but we still have columnists who bring fresh home cooking ideas to readers every week. These are recipes developed specifically for our Bay Area readers, reflecting our tastes and our farmers' markets.

And all now have photos, many of which were made just for this book by photographers Lauren Segal and Andrea D'Agosto.

"San Francisco by Season" is a collection of 67 favorite recipes from the last 10 years, created by regular columnists such as Christian Reynoso, Amisha Gurbani, Jessica Battilana and Nik Sharma, as well as former Food & Wine team staffers like Tara Duggan and Sarah Fritsche. Some were unusually popular with readers when they were first published. Others are loved by past or current Chronicle staffers, who make them regularly. Many have been retested and updated. That means you may recognize a recipe from a few years ago, but it could have clearer, streamlined directions or adjusted seasoning.

Together, these recipes represent how we love to cook and eat right now. We have many vegetarian dishes spotlighting prized farmers' market finds like peas in the spring and tomatoes in the summer. We include multiple Dungeness crab dishes for the winter. Lots of pasta year-round. Spicy curries. Vibrant, meal-worthy salads. Soothing soups. Fruity desserts.

A few notes: With our enviable weather, seasons often blend together, so you might find an ingredient like eggplant in the summer and fall sections. We have several fabulous Indian recipes requiring spices that, depending on where you live, might not be possible to find at your neighborhood grocery store. If you can plan ahead, try these great online resources for quality spices: Burlap & Barrel (burlapandbarrel.com), Diaspora Co. (diasporaco.com) and Oaktown Spice Shop (oaktownspiceshop.com). Even something basic like cumin can taste worlds better from one of these outfits.

Related: The type of salt you use can make a major difference in the final dish. Since these recipes were developed by different cooks, they used different salts. Pay attention to when it says "fine sea salt," for example, versus "Diamond Crystal kosher salt," which has bigger crystals and is far less salty. In some cases, the type of salt doesn't matter because there are no measurements; you're just salting to taste.

Finally, we can't forget about wine. Wine critic Esther Mobley wrote pairing recommendations for 22 of the most wine-friendly recipes. She spotlights a few specific California wineries for each, giving you more to try when you make the recipe again.

SPRING

For the first few years of the nearly 20 that I lived in San Francisco, I believed it was a city without seasons. Having moved from New England, where weather is a near-constant concern and topic of conversation, I found it difficult to mark time in this new place without the familiar environmental cues.

No month of the year was as confusing to me as March. Elsewhere, I knew, the world was a desolate snowscape, a study in gray and brown. Meanwhile, on our block in the Lower Haight, the cherry tree put forth its pink pom-pom blossoms. Sonoma County exploded in a brilliant yellow carpet of flowering mustard. And, marvelous and disorienting, the first Zuckerman's Farm asparagus began appearing on restaurant menus.

My confusion gave way to enthusiasm: At the market, piles of fava beans, mounds of peppery arugula and thin-skinned new potatoes were more reliable harbingers of spring than any calendar. I grilled garlic scapes on my patio in February. In March, I bought bags of English peas, shelled them and ate them raw by the handful. By April, I was scraping my teeth across the petals of a steamed artichoke grown just down the coast.

And if all that wasn't enough, flats of strawberries — sweet and juicy, not tasteless cardboard impostors — arrived, rubbing shoulders with the last of the citrus.

I was wrong: There are seasons, and they are glorious.

There's never a bad time to be a cook in California, not really; every month of the year offers an embarrassment of riches. But when spring makes its start, it may be the very best time of all.

— JESSICA BATTILANA

Artichokes With Green Garlic Bagna Cauda

SERVES 4

Bagna cauda is a potent sauce of garlic and anchovies, traditionally served as a warm dip with winter vegetables in Italy's Piedmont region. For a spring twist, Tara Duggan incorporates green garlic, young garlic plants with a milder flavor that won't overwhelm a pairing of artichokes.

- Salt
- 2 large or 4 small artichokes, trimmed
- ½ cup extra-virgin olive oil
- 4 tablespoons unsalted butter
- 6 anchovy filets
- 3 stalks green garlic, finely minced, including white and light green stalks
- 1 tablespoon lemon zest, preferably Meyer lemon
- Crusty bread, for serving (optional)

Fill a large pot about halfway with salted water and bring to a boil. Add the artichokes, reduce to a simmer and cook, covered, until the artichokes are tender when pierced in the heart with a knife or their outer leaves come off easily, about 20 minutes. Drain upside-down in a colander and let cool briefly.

Heat the olive oil, butter, anchovies and green garlic in a small saucepan over low heat. Let cook, stirring to break up the anchovies, until the flavors combine, about 8–10 minutes. Stir in the lemon zest.

Serve the sauce on the side with artichokes and bread, if using.

Wine paring tip: *The ultra-green flavors of this dish, which utilizes in-season artichokes and green garlic, scream spring. Vegetal flavors can be difficult to pair with wine, and artichokes are particularly notorious thanks to a compound called cynarin, which can make wines taste sweeter than they actually are. So whatever you drink with this dish, make sure it's bone-dry. You might consider a wine made from the Austrian grape Gruner Veltliner, which tends to have green flavors itself: Common Gruner descriptors include pea shoot and green lentil. Gruner is scarce in California, but if you can find the versions from Tatomer, Camins 2 Dreams and Fifth Moon, snatch them up.*

Asparagus With Bacon & Sambal-Lime Vinaigrette

SERVES 4

Reading the title here, you may be thinking, how could this recipe not be good? You would be correct. Christian Reynoso's speedy asparagus dish is spicy, smoky, sweet and tangy all at once. The key is sambal oelek, an Indonesian chile pepper sauce made with crushed chiles, vinegar and salt.

- 1½ pounds thick asparagus spears
- 6–8 ounces slab of bacon (without skin) or pancetta
- Kosher salt
- 2 tablespoons olive oil, plus more if needed
- 2 small shallots, finely chopped
- 1½ tablespoons sambal oelek
- Zest from 1 lime
- ¼ cup lime juice
- 2 tablespoons brown sugar
- ¼ cup chopped dill

Slice or snap tough bottoms off the asparagus spears and discard (or keep to make veggie broth). Slice the bacon into lardons, pieces about ½-inch thick, and set aside. Fill a large bowl with ice water and set it near your stove.

Fill a large skillet (preferably 10–12 inches wide with high sides) with 1½ inches of water and bring to a rapid simmer. Season with enough salt so that you can taste it, but it's not salty. Add half of the asparagus spears in the water and cook them until crisp-tender, about 45 seconds to 1 minute and 15 seconds. With tongs, quickly transfer the blanched asparagus to the prepared ice water bath and swish them around; repeat with the remaining asparagus. Let excess water drip off the spears and transfer them to a serving platter.

Discard the water in the pan, wipe it dry and then heat the olive oil over medium-high heat. Add the bacon lardons and cook, stirring regularly until they are golden and crispy. You still want some chew left, so don't get them too, too crispy. Turn off the heat, and transfer the lardons to the platter with the asparagus. Make sure there are 4 tablespoons of fat in the pan; discard any excess or add more olive oil, if needed, to equal 4 tablespoons.

Turn the heat back on to medium, stir in the shallots and cook until softened, about 1 minute. Turn off the heat and stir in the sambal oelek, lime zest, lime juice and brown sugar until the mixture melts together. Taste and season with salt, if needed. Spoon the sauce over the asparagus, sprinkle the dill over and serve.

Slow-Roasted Salmon Salad

SERVES 4

This Nicoise-esque salad is really an excuse to eat salmon Jessica Battilana's favorite way: coated with herbs and slow-roasted until just cooked. When wild king salmon season kicks off in the spring, keep this preparation in mind — tucking chunks of custardy fish into tortillas or bread are good bets, too. As for the salad, you can make each element in advance, but don't dress it until you're about to eat.

Salad

- 12 ounces salmon (preferably wild king), in one piece
- Kosher salt and freshly ground black pepper
- 2 tablespoons finely chopped chives
- 2 tablespoons finely chopped parsley
- ½ teaspoon lemon zest
- 1 tablespoon extra-virgin olive oil
- 4 large eggs
- 8 marble potatoes
- ¼ pound sugar snap peas, trimmed
- ¼ pound green beans, trimmed
- 1 small head Bibb lettuce
- ⅛ cup finely chopped cornichon pickles

Dressing

- 2 tablespoons finely chopped shallot
- 1 tablespoon Dijon mustard
- ¼ cup apple cider or white wine vinegar
- ½ cup extra-virgin olive oil
- Flaky salt, such as Maldon, for garnish

Make the salad: Preheat the oven to 250 degrees. Fill a baking dish (a 13-inch by 9-inch works well) halfway with water and place on the bottom rack of the oven.

Season the salmon generously with salt and pepper on both the skin and flesh side. In a small bowl, combine the chives, parsley, lemon zest and olive oil. Mix to combine. Smear this paste all over the fish to coat. Transfer to a baking sheet and place in the oven on a rack above the baking dish with water. Bake for about 20–25 minutes, until the salmon is flaky but still very moist. (Use the tip of a paring knife to peek at the interior; it should flake easily.) Remove from the oven and let cool, then break the salmon into large chunks and discard the skin and pin bones (they'll be very easy to remove once the fish is cooked).

While the fish is cooking, prepare the salad. Bring a large saucepan of salted water to a boil. When the water is boiling, add the potatoes and cook until tender, about 8–12 minutes. Remove from the water with a slotted spoon and set aside. Do not discard the water. When cool enough to handle, cut each potato in half.

Fill a large bowl with water and ice.

Add the snap peas and green beans to the boiling water and cook until tender, about 4–5 minutes. Use a slotted spoon to transfer to the ice-water bath. Let stand until cool, then transfer to a paper-towel-lined plate to drain. Cut the snap peas and green beans in half crosswise.

Add the eggs to the boiling water and boil for 7 minutes. Drain and transfer to the ice-water bath, adding more ice if necessary. Once cool, peel the eggs and set aside.

Make the dressing: In a small bowl, whisk together the shallot, mustard, vinegar and about ½ teaspoon of salt. Let stand 10 minutes, then whisk in the olive oil until combined. Season to taste with additional salt.

Assemble: In a large salad bowl, toss the lettuce with some of the dressing to coat. Season the lettuce with salt and arrange on a platter. Scatter the snap peas, green beans and halved potatoes over the lettuce, then top with the chunks of salmon. Scatter the cornichon pickles over. Cut each egg in half and arrange around the perimeter of the salad. Spoon more dressing over the fish, potatoes and eggs, then season the salad with a bit of flaky salt. Serve right away.

Wine pairing tip: *Salmon is the rare fish that can usually stand up to red wine, but the spring produce in this salad calls out for something lighter. Chenin Blanc is a great choice. A wine like the Jurassic Park Chenin Blanc from Paso Robles winery Field Recordings has mellow citrus notes to echo the salad's vegetal brightness, and a sea-salt note that brings out the flavor of the fish. Other fine Chenin makers include Haarmeyer, Leo Steen and Roark.*

Lamb Meatball & Herb Salad

SERVES 4

This is a fully loaded salad with something interesting in every bite: rich meatballs spiced with harissa, sweet sugar snaps, creamy feta, soft herbs and a zingy vinaigrette. Instead of croutons, Jessica Battilana toasts slices of lavash to crumble on top. And while lamb sings here, you could substitute ground beef, pork or a vegan alternative like Impossible Burger. Feel free to prepare the lavash, blanched vegetables and dressing in advance, but don't assemble the salad until you're ready to serve.

Salad

2 pieces lavash bread
3 tablespoons extra-virgin olive oil
Kosher salt
Aleppo pepper (optional)
1 pound ground lamb
3 teaspoons prepared harissa
3 garlic cloves, minced
2 cups sugar snap peas, trimmed
6 radishes, thinly sliced
1 thin-skinned Japanese, Armenian or English cucumber, thinly sliced
1 cup flat-leaf parsley leaves
1 cup mint leaves
1 cup dill fronds
3 scallions, thinly sliced
½ cup crumbled feta cheese
¼ cup sunflower seeds, toasted

Dressing

1 teaspoon Dijon-style mustard
3 tablespoons lemon juice
¼ cup extra-virgin olive oil
Kosher salt

Prepare the lavash: Preheat the oven to 350 degrees. Put the pieces of lavash side by side on an unlined, rimmed baking sheet. Brush each piece on both sides with olive oil. Season with kosher salt and a dusting of Aleppo pepper, if using. Transfer to the oven and bake until golden brown and crisp, about 8 minutes. Let cool, then break into irregular bite-size pieces and set aside.

Make the meatballs: In a bowl, combine the lamb, harissa, garlic and 1 teaspoon of kosher salt. Mix with your hands until well combined. Roll into 1-inch balls. In a large nonstick frying pan over medium-high heat, cook the meatballs, turning with a spoon as needed, until lightly browned on both sides but still slightly pink within, about 6 minutes total. Use a slotted spoon to transfer to a paper towel-lined plate. Let cool until just warm.

Make the snap peas: Bring a medium saucepan of salted water to a boil over high heat and drop in the sugar snap peas. Cook until just tender, about 2 minutes, then drain and rinse with cold water. Transfer to a paper-towel-lined plate and pat dry, then cut each pea crosswise into two pieces. Set aside.

Assemble: In a large salad bowl, combine the meatballs, peas, radishes, cucumbers, herbs, scallions, feta and sunflower seeds. Toss with your hands to combine.

Make the dressing: In a small bowl, whisk together the mustard, lemon juice and olive oil. Season to taste with salt. Pour the dressing over the salad and toss gently with your hands to coat. Top with the crispy lavash and serve immediately.

Steak Salad With Celery, Strawberry & Feta

SERVES 2–3

In the early spring, when you impatiently pick up baskets of strawberries but find they aren't quite perfect, turn to this recipe by Christian Reynoso. Firm berries are actually ideal here, since they'll maintain their texture after a dunk in lemon juice. Trust that they're a lovely, if unconventional, match for seared steak, alongside crisp celery, salty cheese and lots of herbs. Note: You'll want to season the steak at least two hours in advance.

1 pound hanger or skirt steak
½ cup extra-virgin olive oil, divided
Sea salt
3 stalks celery
1½ cups whole fresh strawberries (about 7 ounces), not overripe
½ bunch scallions, thinly sliced
1 lemon, juiced
½ teaspoon chile flakes
½ teaspoon black pepper, freshly ground
3 ounces feta cheese, sliced thin, or Parmesan
1 bunch parsley, leaves plucked

Season the steak with 1 teaspoon sea salt and let sit for at least 2 hours or up to 2 days in advance, uncovered in the refrigerator.

When you're ready to cook, remove the steak from the fridge and rub it with 2 tablespoons of the olive oil. Let sit on the counter to temper.

Slice the celery stalks against the grain and on a ¼-inch bias. (The celery should be green through and through: Avoid dry-looking, white, holey parts of the stalks.) Transfer to a medium bowl. Trim the tops off the strawberries and cut lengthwise into ¼-inch slices. Add the berries to the bowl with the celery along with the scallions and lemon juice. Add the chile flakes, black pepper, feta cheese, the remaining 6 tablespoons olive oil and ½ teaspoon salt. Toss to combine. Let these ingredients marinate.

Heat a large cast-iron skillet over medium-high. Once hot, add the oiled steak to the pan and cook, until deeply browned and a crust has formed, about 4 minutes. Turn the meat over and cook until that side is equally browned and steak is medium-rare. Transfer steak to a cutting board and let rest for 5–7 minutes.

Once rested, add the parsley leaves to the salad. Slice the steak against the grain. Serve the steak with the salad and, if desired, more black pepper and flake salt on top.

Wine pairing tip: *Cabernet Sauvignon is typically a no-brainer pairing with steak, but a wine with that much tannin may taste bitter alongside this salad's tart lemon and underripe strawberry. A lighter red like Pinot Noir, with plenty of acidity and just a little bit of tannin to counter the steak's fattiness, would be a better move here. Anthill Farms, Joseph Swan, Alma de Cattleya and Samuel Louis Smith all produce delicious Pinots that would fit the bill.*

Sweet Pea Risotto

SERVES 4

When Jessica Battilana saw pea puree used as a pasta sauce in Thomas McNaughton's cookbook, "Flour + Water: Pasta," she decided to try it with risotto. As it turns out, the technique unlocks a new level of pea flavor — and paints the risotto a stunning shade of green. While intended to showcase fresh spring peas, the recipe works just as well with frozen. As far as the cheese goes, it's worth splurging on the good stuff.

- Kosher salt
- 1½ cups peas
- 2 ounces pea shoots, plus more for garnish
- 6–7 cups low-sodium chicken stock or vegetable stock, divided
- 1 tablespoon heavy cream, half-and-half or milk
- 4 tablespoons unsalted butter
- 1 small onion, minced
- 2 cups arborio or carnaroli rice
- 3½ ounces Parmigiano-Reggiano, grated (about 1¼ cups grated)
- Freshly squeezed lemon juice, to taste

Fill a large saucepan halfway with water and bring to a boil. Add a few tablespoons of salt.

Prepare an ice bath: Fill a medium bowl halfway with ice cubes and add a bit of cold water. Set nearby.

When the water is boiling, add the peas and pea shoots and blanch for 2 minutes. Drain and transfer the peas and pea shoots to the ice bath; reserve the saucepan. Let stand until cold, then drain. Reserve ½ cup of the peas, then transfer the remainder of the peas and pea shoots to a blender or food processor. Add ¼ cup of the chicken stock and the cream. Blend or process until smooth, then season to taste with salt. Set aside.

Pour the remaining chicken stock into a medium saucepan and bring to a gentle simmer. Return the large saucepan to the stovetop over medium-low heat. Add the butter and, when the butter has melted, add the onions and a few generous pinches of salt. Cook, stirring frequently, until tender and light golden, about 8 minutes (if the onions are browning too quickly, decrease the heat). Add the rice and cook, stirring, until the edges of each grain are beginning to look translucent and the rice is making a "plinking" sound in the pan.

Add a few ladlefuls of stock to the rice. Cook, stirring frequently, until all of the liquid has been absorbed, then add another ladleful of stock. Continue this process, adding more ladlefuls of stock anytime the rice looks dry, until the rice is creamy and al dente (you may use all the stock, or have a bit remaining). As the risotto cooks, monitor the heat and adjust as needed to maintain a gentle simmer. From start to finish, the risotto should take about 30–35 minutes.

Stir in the pea puree, then remove the pan from the heat and stir in the Parmesan and the reserved ½ cup peas. The risotto should be very creamy and fairly fluid, with an almost pourable consistency (this texture is called all'onda in Italian, which translates as "wavy"); if it's too thick, you can add a bit of the remaining chicken stock, if you have some, or hot water to thin. Taste the risotto and season with salt and lemon juice. Divide the risotto among warmed plates or bowls, garnish with pea shoots and serve immediately.

Fettuccine Alfredo With Fava Beans

SERVES 4

Alfredo is a cinch to make at home, so long as you follow a few rules: Don't add cream, use dry pasta and grate your cheese using the small holes of a box grater. (A food processor also works here; just don't grab your Microplane, which will lead to pesky cheese clumps.) Jessica Battilana likes the nontraditional addition of fava beans here, with their bright flavor and buttery texture, but you could try peas instead.

- 12 ounces dry fettuccine
- 1 cup shelled fresh fava beans
- 1 stick unsalted butter, cut into cubes
- 1 cup grated Parmigiano-Reggiano cheese
- Salt and freshly ground black pepper, to taste

Bring a large pot of salted water to a boil. Add the fettuccine and cook according to package directions until al dente. About 2 minutes before the pasta is done, add the fava beans to the water. Drain the pasta and favas, reserving 1 cup of the starchy pasta cooking water. (This is essential: Don't forget!)

Return the pot to the stove and add the 1 cup pasta water. Bring to a simmer over medium heat, then whisk in the cubes of butter a few at a time, waiting until one addition has melted before adding more. When all the butter has been added, gradually whisk in the cheese, until all of the cheese has been added and the sauce is glossy and smooth. Add the fettuccine and favas and, with tongs, toss the pasta in the sauce to coat. At first it will look liquid-y and loose, but give it a moment and it will thicken. Transfer the pasta to a warmed platter, season with salt and pepper, and serve immediately.

Wine pairing tip: *Green spring produce can be difficult to pair with wine, due in part to their bitterness, but fava beans are among the friendliest veggies of the season. Favas taste sweet, nutty and gently green, and in this recipe there's plenty of butter and cheese to accentuate their richness. Rhone-style whites were made for this assignment: Wines made from grapes including Marsanne, Grenache Blanc and Viognier tend to offer creamy, full textures, floral aromas and ripe-fruit flavors. California wines like Bonny Doon's Picpoul, Alta Colina's 12 O'Clock High Viognier and Site's Roussanne would work well here.*

Eggs Rockefeller

SERVES 4

More hours of sunlight means more eggs, which is why the ovals have become synonymous with spring. (If you're splurging on pastured eggs, they also taste richer this time of year.) Here, Jessica Battilana gives eggs the oysters Rockefeller treatment. Think runny egg yolks swirling into creamy spinach, topped with buttery bread crumbs. Baked in individual portions or one larger gratin dish, this is a dish designed for easy brunch entertaining.

- 4 tablespoons unsalted butter, divided
- ½ cup panko bread crumbs
- Kosher salt and freshly ground black pepper
- Two (5 ounce) containers baby spinach (about 12 cups packed)
- 1 small clove garlic, peeled and minced
- ½ cup creme fraiche
- 4 large eggs

Preheat the oven to 425 degrees. In a large frying pan over medium heat, melt 2 tablespoons of the butter. Add the bread crumbs and cook, stirring constantly, until the crumbs are crunchy and deep golden brown, 3–4 minutes. Turn out onto a plate and wipe out the skillet with a paper towel.

Return the pan to the stove over medium-high heat and add the remaining butter. When the butter melts, add half the spinach, then cook, stirring, until it begins to wilt. Then add the remaining spinach and continue to cook, stirring, until all the spinach has wilted. Add the minced garlic and cook for 2 minutes more, then remove the pan from the heat and stir in the creme fraiche. Season to taste with salt and pepper.

Divide the spinach mixture among four individual gratin dishes (or place it all in one 8-inch round or oval oven-proof baking dish). Make a small indentation in the center of the spinach and crack an egg directly into it (or space out four indentations, if using a larger dish). Sprinkle each egg with salt and pepper. Transfer to the oven and bake until the whites are set but the yolks are still runny, 15–18 minutes. Remove from the oven and sprinkle bread crumbs over the top of each serving, dividing evenly. Serve right away.

Cheesy Potato & Spring Pea Tacos

MAKES 15

You won't miss the meat with these vegetarian tacos, which are crunchy on the outside and soft, creamy and cheesy on the inside. Christian Reynoso flavors the mashed potato filling with garlic and sweet English peas (or the equivalent amount of frozen peas), but you could try incorporating other seasonal ingredients year round. If you'd like to make your own salsa, try scaling down the recipe in Reynoso's Pork Ribs in Salsa Verde (page 75). But don't fear making life easier by buying a tub. Look for a refrigerated tomatillo-based salsa.

1¾ pounds small to medium Yukon Gold or German Butterball potatoes
Diamond Crystal kosher salt
1 pound fresh English peas (about 1 cup shelled peas)
6 ounces queso Oaxaca or mozzarella
1 small yellow onion (about 8–10 ounces)
5 garlic cloves, finely chopped
5–6 tablespoons extra-virgin olive oil, divided
15 corn tortillas
Salsa verde, for serving

Cook the unpeeled potatoes by placing them in a large pot, filling the pot with enough water to cover them with about 2 inches of water and salting the water heavily. Cover with a lid, turn heat to high and bring to a boil. Once boiling, turn down to a rapid simmer and cook until the potatoes are soft, giving way to a fork but not falling apart, about 25–30 minutes.

While the potatoes are cooking, shell the English peas (if you're working with fresh peas). Cut the cheese into ½-inch pieces. Roughly chop the onion. Line a sheet pan or large platter with paper towels.

When the potatoes are done cooking, drain them of the cooking water and set them aside. Heat the same large pot or a Dutch oven over medium heat. Add 2 tablespoons olive oil; once the oil is warm, add the onion, garlic and 1 teaspoon salt. Cook, stirring often until the onion has softened, about 3 minutes. Stir in the peas and cook for another 2 minutes. Turn off the heat.

Add the potatoes to the pot and mash them using a potato masher or a blunt-edge wooden spoon until you've mashed all the potato into nickel-size pieces. Add the cheese and stir well, so the cheese becomes melty and both the potatoes and cheese are combined with the peas and onion mixture. Season well with salt.

Heat the tortillas to make them pliable and soft over a medium open flame in batches, or microwave on a plate, covered, very briefly.

Spread ¼ cup of the potato cheese filling on half of each tortilla and fold in half. (Move quickly here so the tortillas don't dry out.)

Heat a large skillet with 1 tablespoon olive oil over medium heat. Once oil is hot and shimmery, add 3–4 tacos to the pan at a time and pan-fry on both sides until golden and crispy, about 3–4 minutes per side. Repeat with remaining tacos, adding about 1 more tablespoon of olive oil in between batches.

Transfer the tacos to the paper towel-lined sheet pan and serve with the salsa verde in a bowl on the side.

Crispy Chickpea Dill Pancakes With Sour Cream

SERVES 4

Even if you don't like pancakes, you should try these savory cakes by Christian Reynoso. With crispy edges and smashed chickpeas for texture, they're brimming with in-season green garlic and loaded with two luxurious toppings: a lemony sour cream and avocado. (Look for Brokaw Ranch's rich avocados at the farmers' market.) If you can't find green garlic, you can achieve a similar effect with the same volume of scallions, plus 2 teaspoons of finely chopped garlic cloves. These pancakes are best eaten immediately, but if you have any leftovers, you can reheat them in a 350-degree oven.

½ cup all-purpose flour
¾ cup chickpea flour
1 teaspoon baking powder
Diamond Crystal kosher salt
2 cups canned chickpeas, drained, with 2 tablespoons liquid reserved
2 eggs
½ cup cleaned and chopped green garlic
½ cup chopped dill, plus 2 tablespoons
6 tablespoons sour cream, plus 4 tablespoons
Vegetable oil or extra-virgin olive oil
1 small serrano chile, seeded and finely chopped (about 1 tablespoon)
1 small lemon, juiced
2 small avocados, split in half and pits removed

Whisk dry ingredients and 1 teaspoon salt in a medium bowl.

Pulse chickpeas in a food processor or smash by hand with a masher in a large bowl, until chickpeas are just about split in half. (In a food processor, this will only take 2–3 quick pulses.) Add eggs, green garlic, ½ cup dill, 6 tablespoons sour cream and 2 teaspoons salt. Keep pulsing until the mixture is combined and the chickpeas are broken into small pealike pieces, about 10 second-long pulses.

Transfer the chickpea mixture to a large bowl. In several additions, slowly add the dry ingredients and whisk until thick, pasty and well incorporated. Lastly, whisk in the reserved chickpea liquid until the paste has loosened, like a watery, chunky hummus.

Heat a large nonstick skillet over medium-high heat. Add about 1 tablespoon of oil. Once hot, measure out a heaping ¼ cup of the mixture and add to the hot pan and oil. Make a roundish shape with a spoon or the bottom of a measuring cup. Cook until several bubbles start to form, the edges crisp and the bottom is golden brown, about 1–2 minutes. Flip and cook until the bottom has begun to turn gold, about 30 seconds to 1 minute longer. Transfer to a serving platter. Continue cooking the rest of the pancake batter like this.

Whisk the remaining 2 tablespoons dill with remaining 4 tablespoons sour cream and serrano chile. Squeeze in enough lemon juice to make it drizzle-able. Season with salt to taste and whisk again.

Serve the pancakes with scoops of avocado and the lemony sour cream drizzled over the top.

Tofu Matar

SERVES 4

Fresh green peas star in Amisha Gurbani's vegan take on an Indian restaurant favorite, Paneer Matar. Instead of cheese, she uses baked tofu. And instead of dairy in the spiced tomato curry, she employs soaked cashews. If you become hooked on this recipe and want to make it all year long, frozen peas will certainly work, too.

- 14 ounces extra-firm tofu
- 1 tablespoon cornstarch
- 1 tablespoon vegetable oil, plus ¼ cup
- ½ cup raw cashews
- 1 cup hot water
- 2 teaspoons cumin seeds
- ½ cup red onion, finely chopped
- ½ cup green onions, finely chopped
- 1 inch ginger, grated
- 3 garlic cloves, grated
- 3 medium tomatoes, finely chopped
- 2 tablespoons tomato paste
- 1½ teaspoons Kashmiri red chile powder
- 1½ teaspoons ground turmeric
- 1 teaspoon ground coriander
- 1 teaspoon ground cumin
- 2 teaspoons garam masala
- 2 teaspoons table salt
- 1 tablespoon granulated sugar
- 1 cup peas, fresh or frozen
- 1 tablespoon dried fenugreek (optional)
- ½ cup finely chopped cilantro
- Naan or cooked rice, for serving

Bake the tofu: Wrap the tofu in a paper towel and place on a cutting board. Place a heavy skillet on top, to drain out the excess water, for about 30 minutes.

Cut tofu into ½-inch cubes. Meanwhile, preheat the oven to 400 degrees.

In a medium bowl, add the tofu and the cornstarch. Toss the bowl two to three times to gently coat the tofu with the cornstarch. Add 1 tablespoon vegetable oil, and continue tossing to coat.

Place the tofu on a baking sheet lined with parchment paper, ensuring the cubes don't touch each other. Bake for about 30 minutes, until tofu is golden brown in color. Set aside.

Prep the cashews: Meanwhile, pour hot water into a bowl, add cashews and set aside for 30 minutes.

Make the Tofu Matar: In a large non-stick skillet, on medium-high to high heat, add ¼ cup vegetable oil. After 30 seconds to a minute, add the cumin seeds. Let splatter for 20 seconds.

Add the red onions, green onions, ginger and garlic, and saute to combine. Cook the mixture for about 4 minutes, until the onions start sweating and turn slightly brown. Add the tomatoes and tomato paste, and mix to combine. Cook for another 2–3 minutes.

Add the onion-tomato mixture to a blender, along with the cashews and water used for soaking. Blend until the paste is smooth.

Reduce the heat to medium, and pour the mixture back into the pan. Add the spices: Kashmiri red chile powder, turmeric, coriander, cumin, garam masala, salt and sugar. Mix to combine. Cook for about 2–4 minutes, covering with a lid, as it may splatter.

Add the peas, stir to combine. Turn the heat down to low. Cook the peas with the lid on, for about 3–4 minutes. Then add the tofu and the dried fenugreek, if using, and stir to combine. Cook the Tofu Matar with the lid on for another 3 minutes. It should look thick and creamy.

Finally, garnish with the cilantro. Serve with hot-off-the-griddle naan or plain rice.

Bacon & Spring Onion Tart

SERVES 4

This savory tart looks special, but thanks to store-bought puff pastry, you can throw it together in about 20 minutes — so long as you remember to thaw the pastry sheet first. If you fall in love, Jessica Battilana notes that the recipe is extremely flexible: Use scallions in the winter instead of spring onions (green garlic, another spring treat, is also lovely here); try ricotta instead of creme fraiche; and get creative with the hard cheese. Just be sure to buy high-quality, all-butter puff pastry, such as Dufour.

- 1 sheet all-butter puff pastry (about 9¾ inches by 10½ inches), thawed
- 2 large egg yolks, divided
- 8 ounces thick-cut bacon, cut crosswise into ¾-inch pieces
- 2 cups thinly sliced spring onions (bulbs thinly sliced, green tops thinly sliced on the diagonal)
- Diamond Crystal kosher salt
- 1 teaspoon fresh thyme leaves
- ⅓ cup creme fraiche
- 1 tablespoon finely chopped chives
- Freshly ground black pepper
- 1 cup grated Gruyere or Comte cheese

Preheat the oven to 400 degrees. Line a rimmed baking sheet with parchment paper or a silicone liner. Unroll the thawed sheet of puff pastry on top. With the tip of a sharp knife, score a ½-inch border around the edge of the pastry, taking care not to cut all the way through. Beat together one egg yolk and 1 teaspoon water in a small bowl. Brush the egg wash on the border, then transfer the dough (still on the pan) to the freezer.

Heat a medium frying pan over medium heat. Line a plate with paper towels and set nearby. Once the pan is hot, add the bacon and cook, stirring, until the fat has rendered and the bacon is becoming crisp, 3–5 minutes. With a slotted spoon, transfer the bacon to the paper-towel-lined plate. Pour the bacon fat into a heatproof bowl, then measure out 3 tablespoons of the fat and return it to the frying pan (if you don't have enough bacon fat, add olive oil to make up the difference). Return the pan to medium and add the onions and a fat pinch of salt. Cook, stirring, until the onions are beginning to wilt, 2 minutes, then add in the bacon and thyme. Continue to cook until the onions are soft, 2 minutes more. Set aside to cool.

In a small bowl, stir together the creme fraiche, chives and remaining egg yolk; season with ½ teaspoon salt and a few grinds of pepper. Remove the pastry from the freezer. Spread the creme fraiche mixture over the pastry, avoiding the edge. Top with the grated cheese, then the bacon-onion mixture. Transfer to the oven and bake, rotating the pan once, until the pastry is golden brown and crispy (use a spatula to lift the tart and check the underside), 22–25 minutes. Transfer to a wire rack and let cool for 10 minutes, then slide onto a cutting board and cut into 8 even squares.

Fish Cakes With Tartar-ish Sauce

MAKES 12 CAKES

Spring marks the start of California halibut season, and the sturdy fish is well-suited to being formed into herb-flecked cakes, coated in bread crumbs and pan-fried until golden brown. Jessica Battilana pairs these fish cakes with a homemade version of tartar sauce, full of pickles, capers and lemon.

Fish cakes

- 3 tablespoons unsalted butter
- 1 medium yellow onion, finely diced
- 1 rib celery, finely diced
- 1 teaspoon Diamond Crystal kosher salt, plus more to taste
- 1 pound boneless, skinless California or Alaska halibut, cut into ¼-inch cubes, divided
- ⅓ cup heavy cream
- 1 teaspoon Dijon mustard
- ½ teaspoon freshly ground black pepper
- 2¾ cups panko bread crumbs, divided
- ¼ cup finely chopped flat-leaf parsley
- 2 tablespoons finely chopped tarragon
- 4 large eggs, divided
- ¾ cup all-purpose flour
- Olive oil, for frying

Sauce

- 3 tablespoons mayonnaise
- 1 hard-boiled egg, finely chopped
- 1 tablespoon finely chopped parsley
- 4 cornichon pickles, finely chopped
- 2 teaspoons capers, finely chopped
- 2 teaspoons lemon juice
- Kosher salt and freshly ground black pepper

Make the fish cakes: In a medium frying pan over medium heat, melt the butter. Add the onions, celery and a pinch of salt and cook, stirring frequently, until softened but not browned, about 10 minutes. Transfer to a bowl and let cool completely.

In the bowl of a food processor, combine ½ cup of the diced fish and the heavy cream and process into a smooth paste. Transfer to the bowl with the cooled vegetables and add the remaining diced fish, the 1 teaspoon salt, mustard, pepper, ¾ cup of the bread crumbs, the parsley, tarragon and 2 eggs. With your hands, mix well to combine. Form the mixture into 12 cakes, each about ¾-inch thick and 3 inches wide. Transfer to a plate or baking sheet and refrigerate for at least 30 minutes or up to 4 hours.

Make the sauce: While the cakes chill, make the sauce. In a small bowl, stir together the mayonnaise, egg, parsley, pickles, capers and lemon juice. Season to taste with salt and pepper.

Finish the fish cakes: Preheat the oven to 300 degrees.

In a shallow dish, pour the flour and mix with a pinch of salt. In a second shallow dish, whisk the remaining 2 eggs with a pinch of salt. In a third shallow dish, pour the remaining 2 cups bread crumbs and season with a pinch of salt. Coat each fish cake in flour, shaking off excess, then dip in egg, letting excess drip off. Dredge in bread crumbs, turning twice and patting to adhere. (Note: It's useful to designate one hand your "dry" hand, the one you use to turn the cakes in the flour and bread crumbs, and one the "wet" hand, the one you use to turn the cakes in the beaten egg. This way, you avoid breading your fingers, too.) Set on a plate or rimmed baking sheet. Set a wire rack over a second rimmed baking sheet and set nearby.

In a large frying pan, heat ½-inch depth of olive oil over medium heat. When the oil is hot, add as many fish cakes as will comfortably fit in a single layer and fry, turning once, until golden brown on both sides and cooked through, about 6 minutes total. With a spatula, transfer the cakes to the wire rack over the baking sheet and keep warm in the oven while you fry the remaining fish cakes, adding more oil to the pan as necessary.

Transfer the fish cakes to a platter and season with salt. Serve warm, accompanied by the tartar-ish sauce.

Mustard-Rubbed Pork Shoulder With Really Green Sauerkraut

SERVES 2–3

What makes this seemingly wintry combination of braised pork and sauerkraut, in fact, a springtime treasure? It's that really green" aspect: Christian Reynoso brightens up the kraut with crunchy raw asparagus and fresh herbs like tarragon. Feel free to scale up the recipe to feed a crowd, as long as you can fit all of the meat in your Dutch oven.

- 2½ pounds boneless pork shoulder
- Diamond Crystal kosher salt
- 2 tablespoons Dijon mustard
- 2 tablespoons whole grain mustard
- 2 tablespoons white wine vinegar
- 3 tablespoons light brown sugar
- 3 garlic cloves, finely chopped or grated
- 12 ounces fresh sauerkraut
- ¼ cup finely chopped tarragon, leaves and tender stems
- ¼ cup finely chopped chives
- 1 cup flat leaf parsley, tender leaves
- ½ bunch asparagus (½ pound)

Preheat the oven to 350 degrees. Place the pork in a Dutch oven and season all over with 2 teaspoons of salt. In a small bowl, add the mustards, vinegar, sugar and garlic. Whisk together well to dissolve the sugar. With your hands, rub this wet mixture all over the pork well enough to fill any pockets. You'll have a little extra rub, which is OK and will flavor the braising liquid, too. Add 2 cups of water; avoid pouring it directly over the pork.

Cover the Dutch oven with a lid and place on the middle rack in the oven. Cook for 1 hour. After the first hour, use an oven mitt to carefully (it's going to be hot!) remove the lid from the pot and use tongs to turn the pork over, then keep cooking for 1 more hour, covered. At the end of the second hour, turn up the heat to 450 degrees and take off the lid. Cook until almost all of the liquid has evaporated, the bottom of the pot is mostly rendered fat and residual mustard marinade, the pork is golden brown and the meat is tender, about 30 minutes. (The total cooking time will be about 2½ hours.) Transfer the pork to a cutting board and let rest for 15 minutes before serving.

During the last 30 minutes of cooking, prepare the sauerkraut. Heat a small pot over medium heat, add the sauerkraut and stir occasionally until it's warm but not piping hot. Turn off heat.

Slice the asparagus on the bias into ¼-inch pieces. Once the sauerkraut is about room temperature, add the asparagus, tarragon, chives, half the parsley and a couple spoonfuls of the rendered pork fat in the Dutch oven. Toss well.

Once the pork has rested, carefully carve into ½-inch slices. Arrange on a platter with the sauerkraut and the remaining parsley leaves over the top.

Wine pairing tip: *The key element in pairing a wine to this dish will be acidity; the sharp mustard and pungent sauerkraut demand a bright wine. While braised pork might typically conjure thoughts of red wine, this particular dish will play better with a white that can harmonize with the crunchy, green herbs and asparagus. Opt for a Sauvignon Blanc, which has acid and herb notes in spades. Lusher versions that display some creaminess — like those from Margerum, Merry Edwards and Groth — should pair better with the meat than a more austere style.*

Parmesan-Crusted Lamb With Minted Spinach

SERVES 2

Perhaps you're looking for a punchy lamb recipe for Easter? Try coating lamb chops in Parmesan and bread crumbs, crisping them up in hot oil and serving over a bed of lush, minty greens. If you're hosting, Christian Reynoso's recipe easily scales up; count on three lamb chops per person.

6 rib lamb chops (about 1–1¼ inches thick)
Salt
Freshly ground black pepper
⅓ cup finely grated Parmigiano Reggiano, tightly packed, plus more for serving
⅓ cup panko bread crumbs or homemade coarse raw bread crumbs
1 egg
¼ cup grapeseed or canola oil
2 tablespoons olive oil
1 large shallot, chopped
6 ounces spinach, roughly chopped
1½ cups mint leaves
Flake salt, for serving
Red chile flakes
1 lemon, cut into wedges

Season the lamb chops with salt and pepper. Mix together the bread crumbs and the Parmigiano Reggiano on a plate large enough to accommodate coating the chops. On another similar-size plate or shallow bowl, whisk the egg until the yolk and white are well combined.

Dip the lamb chops into the egg, making sure all sides including meat and fat have a slick of egg. Let any excess drip off, then press the chop into the cheese-crumb mixture, making sure both sides and edges are coated. Place the coated chops on a sheet pan.

Heat the grapeseed oil in a large griddle pan over medium-high heat. Once hot, working in batches of 3 chops at a time, place the chops into the hot oil. Pan-fry until the crust is golden brown, about 2–3 minutes, then flip and fry the other side until golden brown, about 2 minutes more. Eventually turn the chops on their side and fry until golden brown. (If you're unsure whether the chops are cooked enough, insert an instant-read thermometer into the middle of the thickest part; if it reads 125 degrees, it's medium rare.) Once done, turn off heat and transfer chops to a work surface to rest.

Carefully discard excess oil and wipe the pan clean. Heat the olive oil in the same pan over medium heat. Once hot, add the shallot and saute, stirring often until softened, about 2 minutes. Turn up the heat to high and add the spinach. After about 1 minute, stir and turn the spinach to evenly wilt the leaves. After about 2 more minutes, fold in the mint leaves and cook just long enough to wilt them, about 30 seconds. Turn off the heat and season the minted spinach with salt and black pepper, if desired.

Make a bed of minted spinach on each of the serving plates and place the lamb chops on top. Sprinkle with flake salt, finely grated Parmigiano Reggiano and chile flakes. Squeeze fresh lemon juice over the lamb and spinach. Serve immediately.

Wine pairing tip: *Lamb is almost always an excellent mate for Syrah, thanks to the wine's inherent gameyness. The other ingredients called for alongside these chops only reinforce Syrah's suitability for the recipe: the fresh mint, the umami-packed Parmesan crust, the bitter spinach. So many California Syrahs would be great here, including wines from Pax, Minus Tide, Madson, Darling and the Hilt.*

Baked Rhubarb Custard With Ceylon Cinnamon

SERVES 4

There was a learning curve to using rhubarb for Nik Sharma, who didn't encounter the heralded springtime stalks while growing up in India. Over time, he has learned to make the ingredient his own, dolloping rhubarb jam over yogurt, roasting the red stalks into a rosewater-scented sharbat (an Indian drink) or making it into this custard with fresh-grated Ceylon cinnamon. Milder than the standard cassia cinnamon, grate a stick of Ceylon along a Microplane zester just before using and enjoy the fragrance. If you can't find it, cassia cinnamon will work too; just use a bit less.

- 1 teaspoon unsalted butter
- 1 stalk rhubarb (about 6 ounces), trimmed and thinly sliced
- ¼ cup plus 2 tablespoons sugar
- 2 cups whole milk
- 1 large egg plus 2 yolks
- 1 tablespoon cornstarch
- ½ teaspoon grated Ceylon cinnamon
- ¼ teaspoon fine sea salt

Grease a shallow 11-by-8-inch, or similar-size, baking dish with the butter. In a small bowl, toss the rhubarb with 2 tablespoons of the sugar and transfer it to the baking dish. Let it sit covered for 30 minutes.

Preheat the oven to 325 degrees. Place the baking dish on a baking sheet and roast for 30 minutes until the rhubarb turns plump and releases its juices. Remove the dish from the oven but keep the oven running.

While the rhubarb is roasting, whisk together the milk, egg and egg yolks, the remaining ¼ cup of sugar, cornstarch, cinnamon and salt until there are no lumps. Pour this liquid over the roasted rhubarb in the baking dish and return it to the oven. Bake until the pudding is firm on the sides and slightly jiggles in the middle, about 55–60 minutes.

Let the custard cool in the pan for at least 30 minutes before serving, or refrigerate overnight and serve chilled.

Pistachio-Olive Oil Cake With Strawberry-Rhubarb Compote

MAKES ONE 9-INCH CAKE

This nutty olive oil cake requires no mixer, nor the foresight to soften any butter — no wonder it's become a go-to for Jessica Battilana. She encourages experimentation here: Try a different nut, or lemon zest instead of orange, or a topping of chocolate ganache. But for a beautiful springtime dessert, you'll want to top it with this strawberry-rhubarb compote. (Any leftovers are lovely spooned over ice cream or yogurt.)

Pistachio-Olive Oil Cake

- Butter or cooking spray, for the pan
- 1 cup all-purpose flour, plus more for the pan
- 3½ ounces raw pistachios
- 1½ teaspoons baking powder
- ½ teaspoon baking soda
- ½ teaspoon Diamond Crystal kosher salt
- 1 cup sugar
- 1 teaspoon orange zest
- 3 large eggs
- ½ cup plus 1 tablespoon mild extra-virgin olive oil or pistachio oil
- ⅓ cup plain full-fat Greek yogurt

Strawberry-Rhubarb Compote

- 8 ounces strawberries, hulled and quartered
- 8 ounces rhubarb, peeled and cut into ¾-inch pieces
- 5 tablespoons sugar
- 2 teaspoons lemon juice
- 1 teaspoon lemon zest

Make the cake: Preheat the oven to 350 degrees. Grease and flour a 9-inch round cake pan, and line the bottom of the pan with parchment paper.

Place pistachios in the bowl of a food processor and pulse until finely ground. Measure out ¾ cup and set aside.

In a medium bowl, whisk together the flour, ¾ cup ground pistachios, baking powder, baking soda and salt.

In a large bowl, combine the sugar and the orange zest, using your fingers to rub the zest into the sugar. Add the eggs and whisk until combined, then whisk in the olive oil and yogurt until smooth.

With a rubber spatula, stir the dry ingredients into the wet ingredients until completely combined, then transfer the batter to the prepared pan. Bake until the cake springs back when gently pressed and a tester inserted in the center comes out clean, 30–35 minutes. Do not overbake, or the cake will be dry.

Transfer to a wire rack and let cool for 10 minutes, then run a knife around the edge of the pan and turn out onto the wire rack to cool completely.

Make the compote: Reserve ½ cup of the quartered strawberries. Transfer the remaining strawberries to a medium saucepan and add the rhubarb, sugar, lemon juice and zest. Cook over medium heat, stirring, until the juices begin to release from the strawberries, then continue cooking, stirring, until the juices begin to thicken and the rhubarb has begun to soften, 4 minutes. Reduce the heat to low and continue cooking until the rhubarb is tender and beginning to fall apart, about 2 minutes more. Remove from the heat and stir in reserved strawberries. Cooled compote can be spooned on top of the cake, or served alongside.

Walnut Cakes With Cherries & Whipped Cream

SERVES 6

You don't need us to tell you to eat cherries as much as you can during their all-too-brief season. Given pitting fresh cherries can be a drag, it helps when the rest of the dessert recipe is simple — think clafoutis instead of an elaborate tart, or even simply cherries on vanilla ice cream. These dense little cakes by star pastry chef Emily Luchetti fit the bill, but with their individual servings, they also feel prime for a dinner party. The nuttiness of the browned butter and ground walnuts are a natural but less commonly seen match for the cherries (Luchetti prefers Bing). Don't think about skipping the whipped cream, which brings the whole dessert together.

Walnut Cakes

1 stick unsalted butter
Nonstick cooking spray
½ cup walnuts (pieces or halves), toasted
⅓ cup cake flour
4 large egg whites
¾ cup powdered sugar
3 tablespoons yellow cornmeal
⅛ teaspoon Diamond Crystal kosher salt

Cherries

1 pound (3 cups) sweet fresh cherries, stemmed and pitted
⅓ cup sugar
⅓ cup water
3 tablespoons unsalted butter
Kosher salt

Whipped Cream

¾ cup heavy whipping cream
2 tablespoons sugar
¼ teaspoon vanilla extract

Make the walnut cakes: In a small pot, melt the butter over medium heat, then cook, stirring frequently, until golden brown, 3–4 minutes. Pay attention, because once the butter starts to turn color it cooks quickly. Pour into a bowl and let cool to room temperature while you proceed with the rest of the recipe.

Preheat the oven to 375 degrees. Spray 6 cupcake molds with nonstick spray.

In a food processor, finely grind the walnuts with the cake flour. Set aside.

In a medium bowl, lightly whisk the egg whites until smooth. Sift the powdered sugar into the bowl, and whisk until smooth.

Whisk in the ground walnut mixture, the cornmeal and the salt. Whisk in the room-temperature brown butter. Refrigerate the batter for at least 15 minutes or overnight.

Divide the batter evenly between the cupcake molds. (An ice cream scoop makes it easier.) Bake until a toothpick inserted in the center comes out clean, 15–18 minutes.

Cool in the pans, then remove by inverting the pan and tapping the edge on the countertop. If made ahead, cool completely, then store in an airtight container at room temperature.

Cook the cherries: Place the cherries in a large saute pan with the sugar and water. Cook over medium heat, stirring frequently, until the cherries have begun to soften, about 2–4 minutes, depending on the firmness of the cherries. (Don't cook them so long that they fall apart.)

Stir in the butter and salt, and cook until the butter melts. Turn off the heat and let cool slightly before assembling the dessert. (You can cook the cherries ahead, leave them in the pan and warm them up at the last minute.)

Make the whipped cream: Combine all ingredients, and whisk until soft peaks form. Refrigerate until ready to serve.

To serve: Place a cake upside down on each of 6 serving plates. (If necessary, trim the domed part of the cakes so they will lie flat.) Spoon some cherry juice over the cakes, letting the juice soak in. Spoon some of the warm or room-temperature cherries around the cakes. (If the cherries are too hot, they will melt the whipped cream.) Top the cakes with a dollop of whipped cream, and serve at once.

SUMMER

For me, the farmers' market in the summer is like a candy shop. I want to grab everything I can get my hands on. It's probably my favorite time of year in the Bay Area, full of juicy stone fruits such as plums, pluots, apricots and peaches. And there are tomatoes, melons and berries. And corn, squash, Jimmy Nardello peppers, cucumbers and tomatillos. We are so lucky here to be surrounded by vast varieties of beautiful, vibrant and potent ingredients.

Summer is also a time for easy backyard meals, simple entertaining at home, and big barbecues and potlucks with your loved ones. Luckily, summer produce is so full of flavor that you really do not need to do much with it — simple preparations are key. I tend to use my oven a lot for roasting and turn to my backyard for grilling marinated veggies. Granted, with the Bay Area's microclimates, some don't want to turn on the oven in the summer, while others are usually too cold to imagine grilling outside. Regardless of the temperature where you live, it's hard not to be inspired.

I especially love to make desserts this time of year with fresh stone fruit. One of my favorites is Peach-Chai Tiramisu (see page 83); I roast bright yellow peaches with cardamom and saffron, then layer the mixture with ladyfingers dipped in masala chai and whipped rose mascarpone. On the savory side, my Corn Pakoras With Peach, Nectarine & Heirloom Tomato Salad (see page 55) screams summer in all of its stunning color. Heirloom tomatoes burst with flavor alongside sweet peaches and nectarines; crispy, crunchy corn fritters teem with spices, while a fresh basil vinaigrette ties everything together. It's a crowd-pleaser.

I encourage experimenting with flavor combinations — sour and sweet, or vinegary and spicy — to enhance the produce and make dishes your own. Let the season's bounty shine. Most of all, don't spend too much prep time in the kitchen, so you can maximize the long days with your family and friends. Cheers to summer (I will be lifting Chardonnay)!

— AMISHA GURBANI

Roasted Onion & Poblano Dip With Masala Peanuts

SERVES 6–8

For your next backyard potluck, bring this sweet and spicy take on classic French onion dip. Amisha Gurbani adds a dose of California with roasted poblano peppers and some Indian flair with punchy peanuts. (Find chaat masala, a tart spice blend, at Indian grocery stores or online.) You can make the creamy dip and peanuts a day in advance, garnishing right before serving to preserve the crunch. Either way, serve it with potato chips and whatever fresh veggies look good at the market.

Masala Peanuts

¾ cup raw unsalted peanuts
2 teaspoons olive oil
½ teaspoon table salt
½ teaspoon Kashmiri red chile powder
½ teaspoon chaat masala

Roasted Onion & Poblano Dip

2 large red onions (about 1½ pounds), thinly sliced
3 tablespoons olive oil
1 teaspoon table salt
1 teaspoon black pepper
6 garlic cloves
1 poblano pepper
8 ounces cream cheese
8 ounces goat cheese
½ cup Greek yogurt
1 tablespoon lemon juice
3 tablespoons green onions, finely chopped
3 tablespoons chives, finely chopped, plus 1 tablespoon for garnish
Cilantro, for garnish

Prepare the peanuts: Preheat the oven to 400 degrees.

On a sheet pan, add the peanuts, oil, salt, Kashmiri red chile powder and chaat masala. Mix to combine. Bake in the oven for about 15–20 minutes, until lightly brown in color. Remove and let cool completely. Coarsely chop the peanuts and set aside.

Make the dip: Meanwhile, line a baking sheet with parchment paper. Add the onions, olive oil, salt and pepper. Mix well with your hands until combined. Spread the onions out so that they have space to caramelize. Place the garlic cloves and poblano pepper next to the onions.

Place in the middle or lower rack in the oven for about 40–45 minutes, stirring the onions halfway through.

Remove and cool completely. Chop the onions finely and set aside. Remove the stem from the poblano pepper and, if you prefer no heat, remove the seeds inside.

In a food processor, add the cream cheese, goat cheese, Greek yogurt, lemon juice, roasted garlic and poblano pepper. Process the mixture until completely smooth. Add the caramelized onions, green onions and chives, and mix with a spoon until well combined.

Remove the mixture from the food processor and place in a serving bowl. Create a shallow well in the center, then place the chopped Masala Peanuts in the well. Garnish with chives and a few cilantro sprigs. Serve with crudités and potato chips.

Torn Rice Paper & Pluot Salad With Chile-Lime Sauce

SERVES 4

Look for fruit that isn't overly ripe for this riff on bánh tráng trộn, a Vietnamese rice paper salad. Christian Reynoso likes to tear the stone fruit into chunks, exposing more porous flesh for soaking up a craveable, tangy dressing. Once everything is mixed together, the pieces of craggy rice paper turn into silky strands like magic.

Chile-lime Sauce

5 tablespoons lime juice
3 tablespoons sugar
2 tablespoons neutral oil such as grapeseed, rice bran or canola
1½ tablespoons fish sauce
1½ tablespoons chile sauce such as sambal oelek
3 garlic cloves, finely grated or finely chopped
Salt

Salad

4 pluots or nectarines, or a mixture (ripe, but not too soft, about 1 pound)
2 Persian cucumbers (about 5 ounces)
2 scallions, trimmed
1 cup Sungold or cherry tomatoes
1 large avocado (ripe, but not too soft)
2 small handfuls of small spinach leaves or basil leaves, or a mixture
2 ounces rice paper sheets (about 10 small)
Chopped toasted peanuts or fried shallots, for serving

Make the chile-lime sauce: In a small bowl, whisk all the sauce ingredients, minus the salt, to combine and melt the sugar. Add a pinch of salt to taste, whisk again, and set aside.

Assemble the salad: Halve the pluots, pit them and tear them into smaller chunks, as big or small as you like. Add to a large mixing bowl. Slice the cucumbers and scallions thinly, then halve the tomatoes, and add them all to the bowl. Pit the avocado and, with a spoon, scoop out small chunks and add to the bowl. Add the spinach or basil leaves.

When ready to serve, tear the rice paper into 1- to 4-inch pieces and add to the bowl; folding the round sheets in half first can help break them up easier. Pour the chile-lime sauce over the torn rice paper and then gently toss the salad with your hands or tongs until everything is well-mixed. After 2–3 minutes, the rice paper should soften until tender. Serve immediately with chopped peanuts or fried shallots sprinkled over the top.

Wine paring tip: *The sweetness coming from this salad's stone fruit and sugar-enhanced dressing makes it a tough match for many dry wines. But a light Italian-style white like Vermentino might just do the trick. Often floral, sometimes even a little salty, Vermentino typically has the same level of exuberant fruitiness as a salad that contains pluots or nectarines. Look for California bottlings from Unti, Tablas Creek and Ryme (specifically, the "Hers" Vermentino).*

Corn Pakoras With Nectarine, Peach & Heirloom Tomato Salad

SERVES 6

The Chronicle has published many stone fruit and tomato salad recipes over the years (and even versions with burrata), but this one by Amisha Gurbani is a showstopper. The unexpected addition is pakora, the Indian fritter. Here, they're packed with sweet corn and crispy from a gluten-free blend of chickpea and rice flours. Look for chaat masala, a funky-sour spice blend, at Indian grocery stores or online.

Basil Vinaigrette

1 cup packed coarsely chopped basil, plus more for garnish
3 tablespoons lemon juice
⅓ cup extra-virgin olive oil, plus 1 tablespoon
2 garlic cloves
1 teaspoon Maldon salt, plus more for garnish
1 teaspoon coarsely ground black pepper, plus more for garnish
3 tablespoons finely chopped shallot
½ jalapeño, seeded

Corn Pakoras

2 cups packed corn kernels
½ jalapeño (optional)
1 piece ginger, ½ inch long
½ cup finely chopped red onion
4 tablespoons finely chopped cilantro
4 tablespoons chickpea flour
6 tablespoons rice flour, plus more as needed
1 teaspoon table salt
½ teaspoon red chile powder
½ teaspoon ground turmeric
¾ teaspoon ground coriander
1 teaspoon cumin seeds
¾ teaspoon chaat masala
Vegetable oil for frying

Make the vinaigrette: In a blender, add all the ingredients, except the 1 tablespoon extra-virgin olive oil, and puree on high speed, stopping occasionally to scrape down the sides of the blender. Transfer to a small bowl, and top it off with 1 tablespoon of extra-virgin olive oil and set aside. Clean the blender jar.

Make the pakoras: To the blender, add 1 cup of the corn kernels along with the chile, if using, and ginger. Blend on high speed into a coarse paste.

In a large mixing bowl, combine the rest of the corn kernels, the paste and the remaining ingredients. Thoroughly mix until the batter comes together. You should be able to form balls with your hands. If the dough seems too wet, add a tablespoon or two of rice flour. If it seems too dry, add a tablespoon or two of water.

In a large saucepan or Dutch oven, add about 2–3 inches of oil for frying and heat to 350 degrees. This will take about 5–7 minutes.

Fit a baking tray with a wire rack for draining the excess oil off the pakoras. Set aside.

Scoop out about 2 tablespoons of the batter and form it into a patty, about 1½ inches in diameter. Set it on a large plate or platter. Repeat with the rest of the batter. You should have about 15 pakoras. Working in batches of 3 at a time, to avoid bringing down the temperature of the oil, fry the pakoras for about 1½ minutes on each side, or until golden brown in color. Remove the pakoras with a spider skimmer and place on the wire rack to drain while you assemble the salad.

CONTINUED ON PAGE 56

CONTINUED FROM PAGE 55

Corn Pakoras With Nectarine, Peach & Heirloom Tomato Salad

Salad

4 heirloom tomatoes, cut into half, and then into thirds
2–3 just-ripe peaches, cut into half, and then into thirds
2–3 just-ripe nectarines, cut into half, and then into thirds
2 balls of burrata

Assemble the salad: Arrange the tomato, peach and nectarine wedges on a large platter. Tear each ball of burrata into 3 pieces and nestle the cheese among the fruit. Arrange the pakoras on top of the salad.

Using a spoon, drizzle about ¼ cup of the basil vinaigrette over the salad. Garnish with basil leaves, Maldon salt and coarse black pepper. Serve immediately with the remaining vinaigrette on the side.

Note: *Leftover basil vinaigrette can be stored in a glass jar, in the refrigerator for up to 2 weeks.*

Summer Squash & Corn Tart

MAKES ONE 10-INCH TART

Another showcase of summer's bounty from Amisha Gurbani, this savory tart is packed with fresh corn, summer squash, herbs and cheese. Serve it with a simple green salad on a warm day.

Dough

1⅔ cups all-purpose flour
1 teaspoon table salt
1 teaspoon coarsely ground black pepper
1 stick cold, unsalted butter cut into 1-inch cubes
1 egg, separated
1 tablespoon apple cider vinegar mixed with ½ cup cold water

Filling

1 tablespoon salted butter
½ cup finely chopped red onion
¾ cup corn kernels
½ jalapeño, seeded and finely chopped
½ cup whole milk
1 egg
½ teaspoon table salt
½ teaspoon coarsely ground black pepper
½ teaspoon smoked paprika
½ teaspoon garlic powder
1 tablespoon finely chopped cilantro
1 tablespoon finely chopped chives
1 tablespoon finely chopped oregano
1 zucchini, cut into 1/8-inch thick slices
1 yellow squash, cut into 1/8-inch thick slices
¾ cup grated Gruyere cheese
¾ cup grated fontina cheese
2 tablespoons cotija cheese (optional)

Make the dough: In a large bowl, whisk together the flour, salt and pepper. Add the butter cubes and, using a pastry blender or two butter knives, cut through the butter and flour, until the butter is the size of a pea.

Add the egg yolk (reserve the white), and mix with the pastry blender. Add 6 tablespoons of the cold water-vinegar mixture, setting the rest aside, and work it in with the pastry blender until the dough begins to form.

Empty the contents of the bowl on a clean surface. Using your hands, fraisage the dough, which means to push the dough with the palm of your hand, away from your body, to mix the dough and spread the butter throughout.

If the dough seems dry, add a tablespoon or more of the water-vinegar mixture to bring the dough together. Form the dough into a disk, cover with plastic wrap and refrigerate.

Set aside a 10-inch tart pan with a removable bottom or a 10-inch pie dish.

Dust a clean surface with flour. Roll out the dough, using a rolling pin, into a 12-inch round. Place the rolled dough onto the tart pan and gently press the dough into the pan. The dough will hang over the edge. Tuck it underneath the edge of the pan, working your way around to form a nice ring around the edge of the pan. Place it in the refrigerator for an hour to chill while you make the filling.

Make the filling: In a medium saucepan, on medium heat, add the butter. Once melted, add the red onions, corn and jalapeño. Cook the mixture for 3–4 minutes, until the corn is slightly browned. Cool completely.

In a bowl or large measuring cup, whisk together the milk and egg until combined. Add the salt, pepper, paprika, garlic powder and herbs, and whisk to combine. Set aside.

Assemble the tart: Preheat the oven to 400 degrees. Remove the tart shell from the refrigerator. Using a pastry brush, brush the entire shell with the reserved egg white.

Spread the corn mixture on the bottom of the pan. Layer in half of the zucchini and summer squash slices, alternating between the two in concentric circles.

CONTINUED ON PAGE 58

CONTINUED FROM PAGE 57

Summer Squash & Corn Tart

Garnish

Finely chopped chives
Microgreens

Pour half of the savory milk mixture over the vegetables. Distribute half of the Gruyere and fontina on top. Repeat with the rest of the zucchini and summer squash slices. Pour the remaining milk over the vegetables. Distribute the remaining cheese on the top. Sprinkle the cotija cheese all over, if using. Cover with foil.

Reduce the oven temperature to 375 degrees. Place the pan on a baking sheet and place it on the lowest rack in the oven. Bake for 45 minutes.

Remove the foil carefully, and bake for another 30–45 minutes, until the crust and filling have browned. Remove from the oven, let cool for at least 30 minutes. Garnish with microgreens and finely chopped chives. Serve.

Note: *The leftover tart can be stored in the fridge for up to 2 days. Warm it in the oven before serving.*

Cold Noodles With Tomato-Peanut Sauce, Pork & Peppers

SERVES 4

Chilled peanut noodles are a favorite at many Bay Area Chinese restaurants — and home kitchens. This rendition from Christian Reynoso takes it up a notch, blending peanuts with summer's sweetest Early Girl tomatoes for a bright, garlicky, nutty sauce to coat chewy lo mein. Then he adds browned ground pork for savoriness and another summer highlight: Jimmy Nardello peppers. It's a brilliant combination, and pretty flexible. You could use dried instead of fresh noodles, or bulk Italian sausage — including vegan sausage — instead of ground pork.

---

1 pound fresh lo mein, udon or dried spaghetti noodles
5 tablespoons olive oil, divided, plus more for tossing with noodles
Diamond Crystal kosher salt
1 pound ground pork or sausage
Freshly ground black pepper
½ pound Jimmy Nardello, red bell or other sweet peppers, stemmed and chopped
1¼ cups unsweetened roasted peanuts, divided
¾ pound Early Girl or Roma tomatoes, chopped (about 3–4 large)
5 tablespoons unseasoned rice wine vinegar or lemon juice (or mix of both)
3 garlic cloves, chopped
1 tablespoon fish sauce
½ cup chopped cilantro and/or mint, plus more if desired

Cook noodles in a large pot of boiling water according to package directions. Drain and rinse under cold water, then shake off as much water as possible. Transfer the cool noodles to a large bowl and toss with enough olive oil to coat them. Season with salt and set aside.

Heat 1 tablespoon of olive oil in a large skillet over medium-high heat. Once the oil is hot and shimmery, add the ground pork, using a blunt wooden spoon to break the meat into bite-size pieces and crumbles. Cook, tossing and turning every few minutes, until cooked through and you have a mix of crispy browned and tender bits. Season with salt and pepper, then fold in the peppers and cook, tossing and turning until the peppers are softened and tender but still have a fresh pepper taste (taste a piece or two), about 5 minutes. Transfer to a small serving bowl and let cool before serving.

Place ¾ cup of the peanuts, tomatoes, vinegar or lemon juice, garlic, fish sauce and remaining 4 tablespoons olive oil in a blender, and blend until smooth. Taste, season with salt, pulse, taste again and season again if needed.

Pour the tomato-peanut sauce into the bowl with the noodles and toss very well to combine. The noodles should look fully coated and there should be some sauce pooling at the bottom of the bowl. If there isn't, or if the sauce looks too thick, add a few splashes of water at a time, tossing in-between. Season with salt again and taste until it's sufficiently saucy and delicious.

Chop the remaining ½ cup peanuts. Serve the noodles in bowls with the cooled pork and pepper mix spooned over the top with the chopped herbs and peanuts.

Roasted Eggplant alla Norma

SERVES 4

For a hearty vegetarian entree, Christian Reynoso presents this riff on pasta alla Norma, a famous Sicilian dish where short pasta is cloaked with chunks of eggplant, garlicky tomato sauce and salty ricotta salata. (For a vegan version, omit the cheese.) Instead of pasta, the main attraction here is the eggplant: specifically, slowly roasted, custardy eggplant. If you're wanting carbs, Reynoso recommends throwing a few thick slices of bread in the oven to toast and mop up sauce — after all, the oven is already on.

- 3 medium globe or Italian eggplants (about 2½-3 pounds), sliced in half lengthwise
- ¾ cup olive oil, divided, plus more for serving
- Kosher salt and freshly ground black pepper
- 1½ tablespoons finely grated or finely chopped garlic
- 1 pound tomatoes, chopped
- 1 pound cherry or Sungold tomatoes
- 1 teaspoon crushed chile flakes
- 1½ tablespoons chopped fresh oregano
- Flake salt
- 4 ounces ricotta salata or Pecorino Romano, for serving
- Fresh basil leaves, torn smaller, for serving
- Fresh parsley leaves, torn smaller, for serving
- 4 slices of bread, cut 1-inch thick and toasted, for serving (optional)

Preheat the oven to 425 degrees. Line a sheet pan with parchment paper.

Use a knife to make 3- to 4½-inch slits into the cut side of each eggplant half — try long diagonal slits or X's. Place the eggplant cut-side up on the prepared sheet pan and drizzle with ½ cup of the olive oil. Season with salt and pepper, and then turn the eggplants over so they are cut-side down.

Place the sheet pan in the oven and roast until the eggplants are golden brown on the bottom and the flesh seems very soft when poked with your finger or a spoon, about 35–40 minutes.

While the eggplant is roasting, add the remaining ¼ cup olive oil and garlic in a large skillet over medium heat. Let the garlic sizzle for a couple minutes (but don't let it brown), stirring with a spoon, and then add the tomatoes, chile flakes and oregano. Stir again and cook, stirring every minute or so until the chopped tomatoes sauce out and dissolve, and the cherry tomatoes are super juicy and bursting, with some still intact, about 15–20 minutes.

To serve, spoon some sauce on serving plates, place the eggplant on top and spoon more sauce over the eggplant. Season with flake salt. Shave or crumble the ricotta salata over the top. Garnish with the basil and parsley. Drizzle with more olive oil. Have the toasted bread nearby, if using, for soaking up the sauce.

Wine pairing tip: *For this dish, seek a wine that can match the sweet, garlicky tomato sauce that you'll be spooning on top of the eggplant. A wine with crunchy, red-fruit flavors, like a lighter-styled Grenache, is your best bet. California wineries like Newfound, La Marea and A Tribute to Grace all make fresh, vibrant, translucent Grenache wines that tend toward flavors like raspberry, cranberry and pomegranate, a stark contrast to the heavy style of Grenache that was in vogue for many years. These wines will respond well to a 20-minute chill in the refrigerator.*

Garlic Noodles With Summer Squash & Parmesan

SERVES 4

Vietnamese restaurant Thanh Long is credited as the inventor of San Francisco-style garlic noodles, a favorite pairing for roasted Dungeness crab and now a popular standalone dish on menus all over the Bay Area. For his version, Christian Reynoso combines a lot of butter, garlic and Parmesan with chewy noodles, plus thin ribbons of summer squash for a touch of lightness. Fresh egg noodles are essential here, so seek them out at an Asian grocery store or online. A mandoline slicer will also help you get thin slices of squash that easily wrap around your fork.

- 1 pound fresh egg noodles
- Salt
- 12 ounces small summer squash such as zucchini
- 6 tablespoons unsalted butter, cut into smaller chunks
- 15 large garlic cloves, chopped
- 1 tablespoon fish sauce
- 1 tablespoon soy sauce
- ½ teaspoon ground black pepper
- ½ cup finely grated Parmesan, divided
- Chopped cilantro, for serving

Bring a large pot of water to boil and season generously with salt (about 1½ tablespoons Diamond Crystal kosher or ¾ teaspoon fine sea salt). Cook noodles until al dente, about 3–5 minutes depending on your noodle thickness. Save ¾ cup water and set aside. Drain noodles and rinse lightly with water so they don't stick. Set aside.

Thinly shave the squash into long slices, about ¼- to ⅛-thick. It's best to use a mandoline here, but you can also use a knife to cut the squash into smaller chunks first to make it easier to slice thinly. Transfer to a large bowl and set aside.

Heat another large pot or saute pan over medium heat. Add the butter and, once melted, add the garlic. Stir and cook until garlic is softened, about 2 minutes. Stir in the fish sauce, soy sauce, black pepper, ¼ cup of the Parmesan and ½ cup reserved water. Stir to combine and then turn off heat.

Add the noodles to the saute pan with the sauce. Toss very well to coat and stir in the remaining ¼ cup water, if you want it saucier. Transfer the noodles and any residual sauce to the large bowl with the squash. Add as much chopped cilantro as you like. Toss well to combine and coat each piece of squash with sauce (the squash softens as it sits). Season with salt, if desired.

Serve in bowls with the remaining Parmesan sprinkled over the top.

Wine pairing tip: *The garlicky, salty, buttery nature of this dish will respond well to an effervescent wine, whose carbonation and acidity can cut the richness. Any type of sparkling wine could do the trick, but a petillant naturel — a style that's more rustic and less bubbly than Champagne-method wines — will be especially suitable. The gentle bubbles are a nice match for the summer squash, and if the wine has a little funk to it, all the better to echo the noodles' dusting of savory Parmesan. Cruse, Broc and Carboniste are all masters of the pet-nat form.*

BLT Tostadas With Salsa Macha Mayo

MAKES 6

This twist on the classic summer sandwich puts bacon, fresh tomatoes and greens on a crunchy corn tortilla. What makes Christian Reynoso's recipe extra fun are purslane, with its slightly chewy texture, and salsa macha, the deeply flavored and nutty Mexican chile oil. If you can't find a jar, you could try Chinese chile crisp instead.

6 corn tortillas
6 slices bacon
Canola oil, for frying
12 ounces ripe tomatoes such as Early Girl or heirloom
½ cup mayonnaise
1 teaspoon salsa macha, plus more for serving
1 cup purslane leaves and tender stems or arugula
Salt
1 lime, halved

Heat a skillet over medium and toast the tortillas in batches on both sides until dried out, but not super crispy or crunchy, all the way through, about 2 minutes per side. Set aside on a plate.

Turn the heat up to medium-high, add the bacon slices and cook, turning occasionally, until golden and crisp, about 10 minutes. (Don't go too far: Slightly pliable bacon is a nice textural contrast to the tostada.) Set aside on a paper-towel-lined plate.

Add enough oil to the pan so it's about 1-inch deep. Once the oil is hot (about 325–350 degrees with an instant-read thermometer), fry the toasted tortillas in batches until golden and crisp, about 2 minutes. Transfer to the plate with the bacon and turn off the heat.

Slice the tomatoes into ¼-inch rounds, then set aside. In a small bowl, add the mayonnaise and stir in the 1 teaspoon salsa macha.

To serve, spread the salsa macha mayo on one side of the tostadas, then top with slices of tomato. Season with salt and place bacon on the tomato. Trim the purslane to bite-size clusters, then place on top of the tomatoes and bacon, and squeeze the lime over the top. (If you're using arugula, simply place a bunch on top.) Serve with more salsa macha, if desired.

Wine pairing tip: *This intensely summery dish calls for a summery wine like Albariño. You'll want a wine that tastes crisp enough to balance the tomato's acidity, with a light piquancy to echo the salsa macha. Plus, a cold glass of Albariño is the sort of wine you'll want to keep sipping before and after meals on a hot summer day. There are many great Albariños to try from Spain, but in California some of the finest examples are made by Ferdinand, Hendry and Cadre.*

Braised Chicken With Apricots & Green Olives

SERVES 4

Jessica Battilana didn't intend to reinvent Chicken Marbella, the classic braise from "The Silver Palate Cookbook," when she created this recipe, but that's pretty much what happened. Some of the key changes here are using fresh apricots instead of prunes, which lends brightness and seasonality to the dish, and dousing the bird in significantly less sugar. Think of it as a comforting meal for June Gloom.

- 2 pounds bone-in skin-on chicken thighs
- Kosher salt and freshly ground black pepper
- 2 tablespoons red wine vinegar
- 5 tablespoons extra-virgin olive oil, divided
- 3 cloves garlic, peeled and crushed
- ½ cup all-purpose flour
- 1 large onion, peeled and cut into eight wedges
- ½ cup dry white wine
- ½ cup chicken stock
- 1 tablespoon light brown sugar
- ½ cup green olives, such as Castelvetrano, pitted
- 5 apricots, pitted and quartered
- 2 tablespoons minced flat-leaf parsley
- 1 tablespoon unsalted butter

Season the chicken generously on both sides with salt and pepper. Place in a bowl and add the vinegar, 2 tablespoons of the olive oil and the garlic, and stir to coat. Cover and let stand at room temperature for an hour or refrigerate overnight. (If you refrigerate it, let it come to room temperature before cooking.)

Remove the chicken from the marinade and reserve the marinade. Pat the chicken dry with paper towels. Place the flour on a rimmed plate. Dredge each piece of chicken in flour.

Heat the remaining 3 tablespoons of oil in a large Dutch oven over medium-high heat. When the oil is hot, add the chicken thighs, skin-side down, and cook until golden brown on the skin side, about 5 minutes. Turn and cook on the second side for 2–3 minutes more, until golden. Transfer the chicken to a plate and pour off all but 1 tablespoon of oil from the pan. Add the onion and cook, stirring, until softened and light golden brown, about 5 minutes. Pour in the wine; using a wooden spoon, scrape up any browned bits that have accumulated on the bottom of the pan. Pour in the chicken stock and the reserved marinade. Add the brown sugar, olives and half of the apricots. Stir to mix.

Return the chicken to the pan, reduce the heat to medium-low so the liquid is simmering and cover the pot. Cook for 20 minutes, then uncover the pot, add the remaining apricots and continue cooking for 15–20 minutes more, until the chicken is tender. With a slotted spoon, transfer the chicken, olives, apricots and onions to a rimmed serving platter. Increase the heat until the liquid is boiling, and boil until slightly reduced and thickened, about 3 minutes. Season to taste with salt and pepper, then stir in the parsley and butter, and stir until the butter melts. Pour the sauce over the chicken and serve.

Late-Summer One-Pot Chicken 'Cacciatore' With Peppers

SERVES 4–6

Toward the end of summer, farmers' markets are full of curvy sweet peppers, including the chef-favorite Jimmy Nardello. Cook them down with some hot Calabrian chiles and olives for Jessica Battilana's cacciatore-meets-pepperonata, which you could make with a whole chicken or your favorite parts.

- 1 whole (3- to 4-pound) chicken, cut into 8 pieces
- Kosher salt and freshly ground black pepper
- 3 tablespoons olive oil
- 2 tablespoons tomato paste
- 4 cups thinly sliced sweet red or yellow peppers (or a mixture), such as Gypsy, Marconi or Jimmy Nardello varieties
- 1 large onion, peeled and cut into 8 wedges
- 4 garlic cloves, thinly sliced
- 1 cup chicken stock
- ¼ cup red wine vinegar
- 20 pitted Kalamata olives
- 3–4 whole jarred Calabrian chiles in oil
- 2 sprigs fresh rosemary
- 1 tablespoon unsalted butter, at room temperature
- 2 teaspoons all-purpose flour
- Pasta, polenta, rice or crusty bread, for serving

Generously season the chicken pieces on all sides with salt and pepper (if you think to do this a few hours ahead, so much the better; cover loosely with plastic wrap and refrigerate until ready to cook).

Preheat the oven to 350 degrees. Heat 2 tablespoons of the oil in a large Dutch oven or oven-safe high-sided frying pan over medium-high heat. When the oil is hot, add the chicken pieces to the pan, skin-side down (depending on the size of your pan, you may need to do this in two batches). Cook until the skin is crispy and deep golden brown, 4–5 minutes, then flip and brown on the second side, 2–3 minutes longer. Transfer to a rimmed plate; repeat with the second batch, if necessary.

Add the tomato paste to the now-empty pan and cook, stirring, for 30 seconds. Add the peppers, onions, garlic and the remaining 1 tablespoon oil to the pan. Season with salt and cook, stirring, until the vegetables begin to wilt and soften, 5–6 minutes. Pour in the chicken stock, using a wooden spoon to scrape up any browned bits on the bottom of the pan, then add the vinegar, olives, Calabrian chiles and rosemary. Bring to a boil, then remove from the heat and arrange the chicken pieces, skin-side up, on top of the pepper mixture. The pan should be large enough to accommodate the chicken pieces in a single layer, but they should not be completely submerged. Cover the pan and transfer to the oven.

Bake until the chicken is tender and beginning to pull from the bone, 35–40 minutes. With tongs, transfer the chicken pieces to a rimmed dish and cover with foil to keep warm.

In a small bowl, squish together the butter and flour to make a thick paste. Return the Dutch oven to a burner and bring the pepper mixture and juices to a boil. Drop in the flour-butter mixture and stir vigorously. Continue boiling, stirring, for 3–4 minutes, until the liquid has thickened and reduced slightly. Transfer the pepper mixture to a serving dish and arrange the chicken pieces on top, or return the chicken pieces to the Dutch oven and serve the meal from the same dish in which it was cooked. Serve hot, with pasta, polenta, rice or crusty bread alongside to soak up the juices.

Sungold Tomato & Rotisserie Chicken Enchiladas

SERVES 4

Using store-bought rotisserie chicken makes this enchilada recipe convenient. An unusual saucing of burst Sungold tomatoes — a precious orange jewel of late-summer farmers' markets — makes it feel like a Bay Area original. This rustic, lighter version of enchiladas comes from Christian Reynoso.

- 2 tablespoons extra-virgin olive oil, plus more for drizzling
- 1 medium yellow onion, thinly sliced from root to stem
- 1 teaspoon Diamond Crystal kosher salt or ½ teaspoon fine sea salt
- 6 large garlic cloves, finely grated or finely chopped
- 1 teaspoon red chile flakes
- ½ cup white wine
- 1½ cups chicken stock or water
- 12 (5½-inch) corn tortillas
- 6 ounces mozzarella cheese
- 2 cups Sungold tomatoes, stemmed
- 2 cups shredded rotisserie chicken, seasoned with salt and pepper
- ¼ cup fresh oregano leaves, plus more for serving
- Flake salt, to taste

Heat the oven to 400 degrees. Heat a large saute pan over medium-high. Add the 2 tablespoons of olive oil to the pan followed by the onion and the kosher salt. Saute, stirring regularly until very soft, but not translucent, about 8–10 minutes. Stir in the garlic and chile flakes and saute until aromatic, about 30 seconds. Add the wine and stock, bring to a simmer and then turn off heat. Pour the onion broth into a bowl.

Heat the tortillas over the stovetop in a pan over medium heat (if you have a gas stove, directly over flame to get some nice charred spots) until pliable and soft. Transfer to a plate and cover with another plate so they don't dry out. Set aside.

Tear or slice the cheese into small, nickel- to quarter-size pieces. Set half aside for topping the enchiladas right before baking.

Set up your workstation, having your onion broth, tortillas, non-reserved cheese, shredded chicken, a plate and a 9-by-13-by-2-inch baking dish in front of you. Individually dip one tortilla at a time into the onion broth, set on the plate and then fill the center with about ¼ cup of chicken, some of the non-reserved cheese and some oregano, and roll into a cylinder. Place in the center of the baking dish to start forming a row. Repeat with the remaining tortillas, chicken, cheese and oregano. Pour the remaining onion broth into the baking dish with the enchiladas.

Place the tomatoes on the sides and over the top of the enchiladas, and sprinkle the reserved cheese on top. Generously drizzle olive oil over, sprinkle with flake salt and bake for 30 minutes. The tomatoes should be bursted and slightly blistered, and the cheese melted with some light golden spots.

To serve, use a wide spatula to transfer to plates and sprinkle with more fresh oregano leaves.

Wine pairing tip: *Roasted tomatoes, melty mozzarella and oregano make these enchiladas the sort of dish that could pair well with a range of wines, but a light, rustic Italian-inspired red should perform especially well. Barbera, a grape variety grown throughout Italy, tends to be juicy and berry-forward, with high acidity and low tannins. In other words, it's extraordinarily food-friendly. In California, Barbera has become a specialty of wineries in the Sierra foothills (Forlorn Hope makes a great one), though Idlewild's Mendocino County Barbera and Giornata's Paso Robles Barbera are excellent, too.*

Pork Ribs in Salsa Verde

SERVES 4–6

These baked-and-broiled ribs are ideal for stubbornly chilly San Francisco summer evenings, a burst of brightness when the fog persists. The main character here is the tomatillo, an essential Mexican ingredient. Here, Christian Reynoso slathers ribs in lots of fresh tomatillo salsa — think chile verde — and then serves them with even more salsa.

- 2 racks baby back ribs (about 2½ pounds each)
- 2 pounds tomatillos, husks removed and quartered
- 1 cup white onion, coarsely chopped
- 3 garlic cloves
- 1–2 serrano chiles (depending on how spicy you like salsas), coarsely chopped
- 2 cups packed chopped cilantro leaves and tender stems, plus more for serving
- 3 limes
- Diamond Crystal kosher salt

Place one rack in the middle of the oven; if your broiler is the main cabin of the oven, place another in the upper third of the oven. Preheat the oven to 325 degrees. Line a rimmed sheet pan with a double layer of aluminum foil.

Place the ribs on the prepared sheet. If the concave side of your ribs still has its papery membrane intact, remove it by prying it up at the end of the bones using the tip of a meat thermometer or butter knife, then pull it off with your hand.

To make salsa verde, place the tomatillos, onion, garlic, serrano, cilantro and juice of 1 lime into a blender. Pulse, pressing the mixture down if needed, until you have a smooth but thick salsa. You should have about 4 cups total. Divide the salsa into 2 separate bowls. Season one of the bowls of salsa with salt to taste, then cover with plastic and place in the fridge. Season the second bowl of salsa more heavily (this will season the pork, too) with about 2 tablespoons Diamond Crystal kosher salt (if using table salt or fine sea salt, cut the amount to 1 tablespoon).

Cut the rib racks in half to make 4 smaller racks and place them on the prepared sheet, meat side down. Pour the highly seasoned salsa verde over the racks. Use your hands to massage the salsa into the ribs, then rinse off your hands. Cover the ribs completely and tightly with foil.

Place the ribs on the middle rack of the oven and bake until the meat is very tender, about 2 hours. If your ribs are smaller, they'll take less time; if they're bigger, more.

Carefully take the ribs out of the oven, remove the foil and turn the ribs over so the meaty sides are facing upward. Dip a brush into the extra salsa juices on the sheet pan and generously brush those juices on the ribs.

Heat the broiler and place the sheet pan with ribs underneath. Broil, carefully brushing more juices onto the ribs halfway through, until browned and caramelized in spots and the salsa has formed a golden-brown crust. This could take anywhere from 5–12 minutes. (Really, it depends on how powerful your broiler is and how close your meat is to it; it could take longer, more brushing and adjusting your pan and ribs to ensure they brown evenly.) Take the ribs out of the oven and transfer them to a cutting board.

To serve: Slice between the ribs to separate, and slice the remaining limes into wedges. Arrange on a platter with extra cilantro and the remaining 2 cups of salsa verde.

Wine pairing tip: *Since the flavor of the tomatillo salsa dominates this dish, pick a wine that will pair well with its herbaceous, tangy flavors — say, a dry rosé. The grapes for many rosé wines are harvested early in the season, when their flavors are still tart, sometimes even underripe-tasting, which makes these pink wines a great mate for highly acidic dishes and assertive herbs. You can find high-quality, dry, affordable rosés from practically every corner of California these days; dependable options include Ernest, Mathis and Lucy.*

Spiced Lamb Kebabs With Cucumber Raita

SERVES 6

Summer is grilling season, and this lamb kebab recipe from Nik Sharma offers a quick way to bring smoky, charred meat to your table — as long as you remember to marinate the lamb in advance. The unusual addition to the spice blend here is juniper berries, which add impressive complexity. Be sure to trim as much fat as you can from the lamb shoulder, or ask your butcher to do it for you, so the kebabs are easier to eat.

Cucumber raita

1 large cucumber
2 cups plain unsweetened yogurt
¼ cup chilled water
¼ teaspoon cayenne pepper
½ teaspoon table salt
½ teaspoon black pepper powder

Kebabs

1 teaspoon cayenne pepper
1½ tablespoons dried juniper berries
8–10 black peppercorns
1½ teaspoons coriander seeds
1 teaspoon cumin seeds
1½ teaspoons sea salt
2-inch piece peeled ginger root
4 garlic cloves
1½ cups diced white onions
¼ cup freshly squeezed lemon juice
¼ cup olive oil, plus more for brushing
2 pounds boneless lamb shoulder, fat trimmed and cut into 1-inch cubes
1–2 tomatoes, cut in half
1 lemon
1 tablespoon fresh cilantro

Make the cucumber raita: Trim the top and bottom of the cucumber and slice it in half across its length. Using a tablespoon, scoop out the seeds from the center and discard. Dice the cucumber into chunks and set aside. In a medium mixing bowl, lightly whisk the remaining ingredients; taste and adjust seasoning if necessary. Fold in the cucumber and chill covered in the refrigerator for at least 30 minutes before serving.

Make the kebabs: Coarsely grind all the dry spices: cayenne, juniper, peppercorns, coriander, cumin and salt. (I like to use a mortar and pestle, just to crack the seeds open.) Add this mixture to a blender, along with the ginger, garlic, onions, lemon juice and olive oil. Pulse for a few seconds until you get a smooth paste. Transfer this marinade into a large mixing bowl containing the chunks of lamb. Coat the lamb evenly with the marinade, cover and refrigerate overnight, or at least 4 hours.

When ready to grill, thread lamb onto skewers. Cook on a charcoal or gas grill at high heat, rotating the skewers every 2–3 minutes, until the lamb is cooked to the desired level — I prefer medium-rare, about 10–12 minutes total. Once cooked, place the skewers on a tray and allow to rest covered with foil. Brush each side of the tomato with olive oil and grill on each side for about 4–5 minutes. Remove from heat.

Garnish the hot lamb kebabs with cilantro and a little freshly squeezed lemon juice. Serve with grilled tomatoes and cucumber raita.

Cantaloupe 'Soft Serve'

SERVES 6

You don't need a fancy machine to make this lush, airy, soft serve-esque dessert. Christian Reynoso devised a fast, unconventional method for achieving frozen-treat bliss at home: He chops fresh fruit into bite-size pieces, freezes them and then blends them with powdered sugar and some kind of milk. Try this version with juicy summer melon, then experiment with all of your favorite summer fruit. Just be sure to serve soon after blending, otherwise the mixture will turn hard and icy.

4 cups frozen ½-inch chunks of very ripe cantaloupe
1 cup full-fat coconut cream
2 tablespoons lime juice
6 tablespoons powdered sugar
½ teaspoon Diamond Crystal kosher salt
¾ cup store-bought candied almonds or cashews, roughly chopped

Chill serving bowls in the freezer. In a high-powered blender or food processor, add the cantaloupe, coconut cream, lime juice, sugar and salt. Pulse until the cantaloupe looks like tiny pieces, then blend or process until smooth and airy, about 3–4 minutes, stopping to scrape down the sides as needed.

Serve immediately in chilled bowls with the candied nuts on top. If the soft serve needs to firm up a bit more, transfer it to a container with a lid or a standard loaf pan, covered with plastic, and place in the freezer to chill for a few hours at most.

Blueberry-Lime Cheesecake Bars

MAKES 18

Jessica Battilana doesn't care for New York-style cheesecake, tall and dense and too often topped with canned cherry gloop. So she shocked herself when she loved these cheesecake bars. There's a higher crust-to-filling ratio, and said filling is lighter and tangier thanks to a dose of creme fraiche. Then they get finished with a seasonal blueberry compote, not too sweet and brightened with lime. Bring them to a summer potluck and watch them disappear. Note: To get graham cracker crumbs, pulse graham crackers in a food processor or crush them with a rolling pin in a sealed plastic bag.

Crust

- 2 cups (from 18 sheets) graham cracker crumbs
- ¼ cup granulated sugar
- ½ cup unsalted butter, melted
- Pinch kosher salt

Cheesecake

- 2 (8-ounce) packages cream cheese, at room temperature
- ½ cup creme fraiche or sour cream
- ½ cup plus 1 tablespoon granulated sugar
- 2 large eggs
- Zest of 1 lime
- ¼ cup lime juice

Blueberry Topping

- 4 cups blueberries
- 6 tablespoons granulated sugar
- 1 teaspoon lime zest
- 1 tablespoon lime juice
- Pinch kosher salt

Make the crust: Preheat the oven to 325 degrees. Line the bottom and sides of a 9-by-13-inch baking pan with 2 sheets of foil, crisscrossed, leaving a 2-inch overhang on all sides.

In a medium bowl, combine the graham cracker crumbs, sugar, butter and salt. Mix with a fork until evenly combined. Dump the crumbs into the prepared pan and press into a thin, even layer using your fingertips or the bottom of a glass. Bake for 10 minutes.

Make the cheesecake: In a food processor, combine the cream cheese, creme fraiche and sugar, and process until smooth. Add the eggs, lime zest and juice, and process until combined. Pour the mixture over the parbaked crust and use an offset spatula to spread into an even layer. Return to the oven and bake until set (it should not jiggle in the center), about 25 minutes. Remove from the oven and let cool slightly.

Make the blueberry topping: While the cheesecake bakes, make the blueberry topping. In a medium saucepan over medium heat, combine the blueberries, sugar, lime zest and juice, salt and 2 tablespoons of water. Cook, stirring gently, until the blueberry juices begin to run and thicken, about 6 minutes.

To finish: Pour the warm compote onto the warm cheesecake bars, and with an offset spatula spread into a thin, even layer. Let the bars cool to room temperature, then refrigerate until cold, at least 2 hours or up to overnight. To serve, use the overhanging foil to lift the cheesecake bars from the pan. Transfer to a cutting board and, using a sharp knife, cut into 2-inch by 3-inch bars. You should be able to get 18.

Peach-Chai Tiramisu

SERVES 6

Start with an Indian twist on tiramisu, soaking ladyfingers in masala chai and adding rose water to mascarpone. Then give it a hefty dose of summer with peaches roasted with cardamom and saffron. All together, this dessert from Amisha Gurbani is bold, distinctive and celebratory — and one you can prepare a day ahead.

Masala Chai

½ stick cinnamon
5 cloves
8 black peppercorns
3 cardamom pods
1 star anise
1 piece ginger, ½-inch long
2 cups water
1 tablespoon loose-leaf black tea
⅓ cup granulated sugar

Roasted Peaches

4 small to medium peaches, chopped
2 tablespoons granulated sugar
1 teaspoon freshly ground cardamom
¼ teaspoon saffron
1 tablespoon unsalted butter, melted and cooled

Cream Mixture

1 cup heavy cream, chilled
½ cup powdered sugar
1½ teaspoons vanilla extract
1 teaspoon rose water
8 ounces mascarpone, cold

Layers

12 lady fingers, such as Savoiardi
3 tablespoons dark rum (optional)
2 peaches, 1 diced into tiny cubes, 1 cut into thin slices
¼ cup raw pistachios, finely ground into a powder
Edible gold leaf (optional)

Make the Masala Chai: Add all the whole spices to a mortar and coarsely grind them to release the oils. Add the ginger to the mixture and grind again. Set it aside.

In a medium pan, on medium to high heat, add the water and bring to a boil. Next add all the spices and boil for 1 minute.

Stir in the black tea and granulated sugar, and boil the mixture for 3–4 minutes. Remove from heat. Strain the mixture through a fine sieve into a container. Let it cool completely.

Roast the peaches: Preheat the oven to 420 degrees. In a quarter sheet pan, add the peaches, granulated sugar and cardamom. Lightly crush the saffron between your fingers and mix it in. Add the butter. Toss it to mix well.

Place the tray in the middle rack of the oven and bake for 20–22 minutes, tossing the mixture around halfway through. Once the peaches are roasted, let the mixture cool completely. Using a rubber spatula, lightly press the peaches to create a slightly mushy texture.

Make the cream mixture: In the bowl of a stand mixer, with a whisk attachment, add the heavy cream, powdered sugar, vanilla extract and rose water. Whisk for about 2 minutes, until the heavy cream reaches soft peaks. Do not over whip. Add the mascarpone, and whisk until just combined. Remove all the cream mixture off the whisk attachment and into the bowl. Then add the roasted peaches mixture and fold in with a rubber spatula, to evenly distribute throughout. Spoon the cream mixture into a 16-inch pastry bag attached with a round tip. Seal the top and set aside.

Assemble: Set aside six 6- to 8-ounce glasses. Add the dark rum, if using, to the Masala Chai. Set the lady fingers nearby.

Pipe a layer of the cream mixture into the bottom of each glass. Smooth it with a small rubber spatula. Quickly dip a lady finger into the chai mixture, break into half and quickly dip again. Place the halves, side by side, into the glass. Repeat for the remaining 5 glasses.

Pipe a layer of the cream mixture on top of the lady fingers in each glass. Smooth with the spatula. Distribute the finely chopped peaches evenly into each glass. Repeat the process with the lady fingers for all 6 glasses.

Pipe a final layer of the cream mixture on top of the lady fingers in each glass. Smooth the tops with an offset spatula. Chill the tiramisu cups for at least 6 hours and up to overnight.

To serve: Just before serving, sprinkle the pistachio powder on top. Garnish with the sliced peaches and edible gold leaf, if desired.

FALL

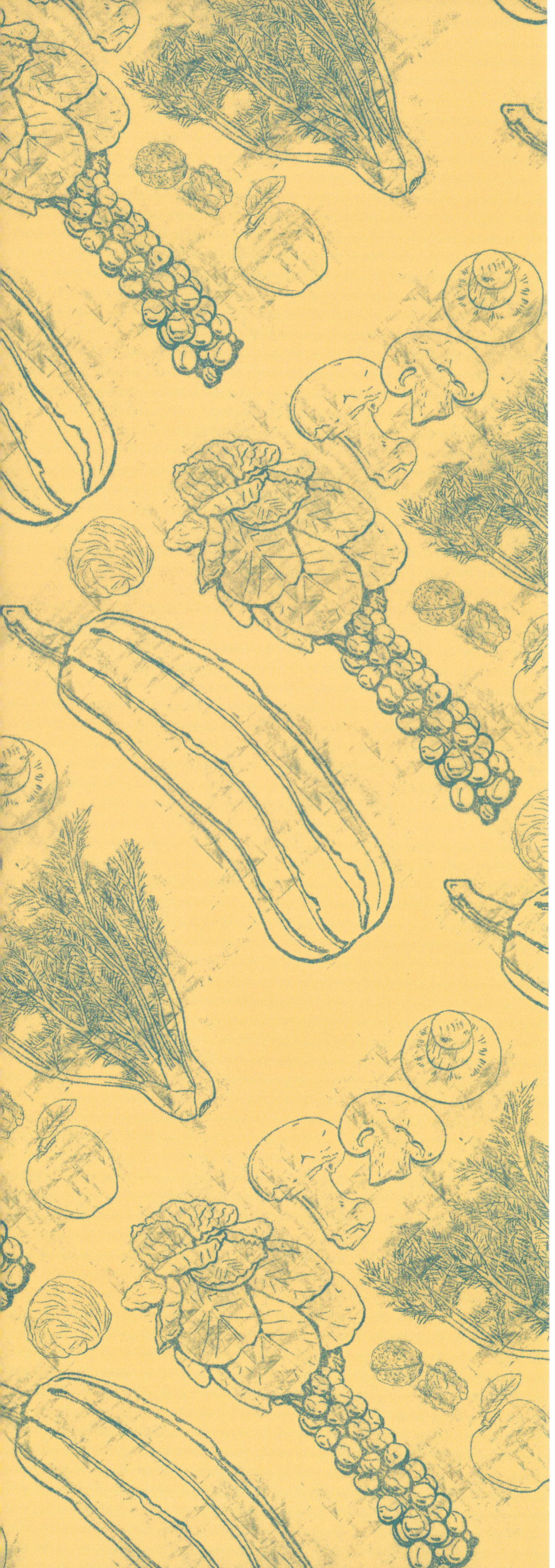

As someone who moved from the East Coast to California, I know fall isn't frighteningly chilly. In fact, the early months can be the warmest all year in San Francisco. Still, by the end, it's time to reach out for a sweater and blanket as you watch the garden transform. The lush green canopy of the sycamore starts to turn golden yellow, the big pineapple-shaped fruit on the quince tree is ready for picking, and figs turn ripe and soft, almost to the point of being squished between my fingers. Then there's the one pumpkin plant that's managed to survive and produce two large rotund squashes that will make their way into a soup or roast. The options on what to cook are endless.

Seasonality has a way of defining our cooking styles. Sure, the produce plays a significant role in what and how I cook, but the lower temperatures also move me toward my oven. I'll try to cook more than one dish in the oven simultaneously on different racks. If I can find an excuse to heat the outdoor pizza oven, I'll jump in and fire it up. I find herbs tend to shine more prominently in the cooler months — I love the piney scent of rosemary dipped into olive oil to brush food before it goes onto the grill and the spicy aroma of the curry leaves as they crinkle in the pan. Warmer aromatic spices take center stage this time of year, and their fragrance takes over the kitchen.

While there is a heavy focus on the big Thanksgiving holiday, this is a beautiful season to entertain regardless. I enjoy the entire process, from creating the menu to picking napkins, tablecloths and floral arrangements. These little things make the meal more memorable. Fall's warmer flavor is a cook's dream, full of vigor, joy and vibrancy.

— NIK SHARMA

Crunchy Apple & Fennel Salad With Cheddar

SERVES 4–6

Apples with cheddar is a classic pairing. Here, Christian Reynoso lets it shine in a bright, sweet-salty salad full of crunch. There's thinly sliced fennel, a lemony vinaigrette, lots of fresh herbs and, of course, sweet apple and rich, aged white cheddar. The salad plays nicely next to a roasted bird, perhaps as part of a certain holiday spread.

- ¼ cup lemon juice
- 1 tablespoon white wine vinegar
- 2 tablespoons honey
- ½ cup extra-virgin olive oil
- Salt
- Freshly ground black pepper
- ¼ cup thinly sliced scallions
- 3 apples such as Sierra Beauty, Pink Lady or Granny Smith
- 2 medium fennel bulbs, removed of their stalks and fronds (about 1 pound)
- ¼ cup roughly chopped dill
- ½ cup parsley leaves
- 2–3 ounces aged white cheddar

In a large bowl, add the lemon juice, vinegar, honey and olive oil. Whisk well to incorporate the honey and then season with salt and as much black pepper as you'd like. Whisk well again, add the scallions and set aside.

Cut the apples into ¼-inch slices and add to the bowl with the vinaigrette. Stand one of the fennel bulbs with the root-side down and make a small vertical slice on the narrow edge to create a flat surface. Then put the fennel flat (cut-side) down and cut into ½-inch strips, starting from the top of the bulb. Pop the fibrous center circles out and discard. Place the fennel strips in the bowl with the vinaigrette and repeat with the remaining bulb. Toss the apple and fennel well with the vinaigrette.

To serve, add the herbs to the bowl, toss well and pile handful upon handful into a sturdy tall mound. Very thinly shave the cheddar over the salad with a peeler.

Wine pairing tip: *Fennel is a strong flavor best paired with a strongly aromatic wine. Pinot Gris or, as it's known in Italy, Pinot Grigio would be an excellent option here, with its lush fruit smells and flavors and relatively light body. But you could also choose a dry white with even flashier aromas, like Malvasia (look for the still and sparkling versions from Birichino) or Muscat (like the one from Margins).*

Celery Salad a la Daytrip

SERVES 2

At the Oakland restaurant Daytrip, you'll spot an unassuming celery salad on just about every table. It's surprisingly elegant, light yet rich, with layers of crunchy celery, spicy habanero aioli, shaved salty cheese and vibrant lemon verbena oil. Christian Reynoso came up with this simpler homage, which serves four as an appetizer, using dried lemon verbena (try ordering it online or visiting San Francisco's Rainbow Grocery) and store-bought Japanese mayonnaise. Use any leftover habanero aioli in a sandwich and extra lemon verbena oil in a vinaigrette.

- 1 cup neutral oil, such as rice bran, grapeseed or canola oil
- 1 ounce dried lemon verbena or 2 ounces fresh lemon verbena leaves
- 1 lime, zested
- 1 large lemon, zested (save lemon for juice below)
- ½ cup Kewpie mayonnaise or another high-quality store-bought mayonnaise
- 3½ tablespoons fresh lemon juice, divided (from about 1 large lemon)
- 1 small habanero chile, stemmed, seeded and minced
- 2 teaspoons Diamond Crystal kosher salt or 1 teaspoon fine sea salt, plus more to taste
- 2 cups thinly sliced celery (from about 5 large stalks)
- ½ cup parsley leaves, lightly packed
- Sheep's milk cheese aged 3–6 months, such as Pecorino Romano or Fiore Sardo, for serving

Make the lemon verbena oil: In a small pot, heat the oil over medium to 190 degrees — use an instant-read thermometer to make sure you reach this temperature, then quickly turn off the heat and stir in the lemon verbena, lime zest and lemon zest. Cover with a lid and let steep for 20 minutes, then strain through a small strainer or cheesecloth into a serving bowl. Set aside while you make the habanero aioli.

Make the habanero aioli: In a small bowl, add the mayonnaise, ½ tablespoon lemon juice and habanero chile, and stir to combine. Taste the aioli (it should be really spicy!) and season with a small pinch of salt, if desired. Transfer to the refrigerator and cover until ready to use.

Make the celery salad: In a medium bowl, toss together the celery, parsley and 2 teaspoons kosher salt. Set aside for a few seconds. Add the remaining 3 tablespoons lemon juice, toss again and set aside for 30 seconds (the celery will start to wilt if it sits any longer).

On a serving plate, spread half of the habanero aioli in a 4-inch circle in the center. With your hand, lift up the celery salad mixture, letting any excess liquid drip back into the bowl, and place the mixture on top of the aioli in a flat circle so it fully covers the aioli.

Thinly shave the sheep's milk cheese over the top of the salad — "make it rain" as they say, adding as much as you desire. (At Daytrip, cheese blankets the salad in its entirety.) Drizzle the lemon verbena oil over the top and serve immediately.

Verde Panzanella With Feta & Walnuts

SERVES 4

Leave it to Christian Reynoso, a former Zuni Cafe chef, to come up with this crave-worthy yet low-maintenance bread salad. You'll toss toasted bread chunks with a surprising pesto made of pungent, peppery broccoli rabe; in-season walnuts and creamy feta. And then you'll immediately want to make it again. He recommends trying it as a simple lunch salad with a fried egg, or as a side to rotisserie chicken.

½ cup mild olive oil, divided, plus more for drizzling
4 slices of bread, 1–1½ inches thick, from something like a country-style loaf
1 bunch broccoli rabe (6–8 ounces), stems and leaves separated
2 garlic cloves
¼ cup lemon juice, plus more for dressing greens
⅔ cup toasted walnut pieces, divided
½ jalapeño, stemmed and seeded
¼ cup oregano leaves
2 cups parsley leaves
4 ounces feta cheese, divided
Diamond Crystal kosher salt
Red chile flakes, for finishing

Put on a medium pot of salted water to boil. Meanwhile, heat a 9-inch skillet over medium heat and add 2 tablespoons of olive oil. Once warm, place two slices of bread down. Toast the bread until crispy and golden-brown with some light char (uneven toasting is basically OK here), about 5–7 minutes. Flip and cook the other side until just warmed and lightly toasted, about 2 minutes. Repeat with 2 more tablespoons of olive oil and the remaining 2 slices.

Add the broccoli rabe stems to the boiling water and cook until crisp-tender, about 2 minutes. Run under cold water, then squeeze out extra water and transfer to a food processor or blender. Next, blanch the broccoli rabe leaves and cook until tender, about 1 minute. Run under cold water, squeeze out any excess water and transfer to a large bowl. Gently unfurl the leaves and set aside.

Finely grate the garlic into the food processor, then add the ¼ cup lemon juice, ⅓ cup walnuts, jalapeño, oregano, parsley, 3 ounces of the feta, the remaining ¼ cup olive oil and ½ teaspoon salt. Pulse until smooth. Taste and season with salt again, if needed. Transfer the pesto to a bowl.

Tear the toasted bread into 2-inch chunks and add to the bowl with the broccoli rabe. Add a little more lemon juice, a generous drizzle of olive oil and salt to taste. Toss well.

Place the torn croutons and broccoli leaves on a platter, spoon the pesto over and sprinkle with the remaining walnuts, feta and chile flakes. Drizzle more oil if desired.

Tandoori Brussels Sprouts

SERVES 6

Give roasted Brussels sprouts a jolt of flavor with Indian spices, crunchy walnuts and sweet-tart pomegranate seeds, courtesy of Amisha Gurbani. You can use store-bought tandoori masala, a spice blend typically used with yogurt to marinate meat, or make Gurbani's shortcut version.

Tandoori Masala

1 tablespoon cumin seeds
1 tablespoon coriander seeds
2 teaspoons fennel seeds
1 tablespoon and 2 teaspoons garam masala
1 tablespoon Kashmiri red chile powder
1 teaspoon red chile powder (optional, if you like it a bit spicy)
1 tablespoon and 1 teaspoon smoked paprika
2 teaspoons ground turmeric
2 teaspoons garlic powder
2 teaspoons ground ginger
3 teaspoons chaat masala
1 heaping tablespoon dried fenugreek

Brussels sprouts

¼ cup olive oil
2 tablespoons Tandoori Masala
1½ teaspoons table salt
1½ pounds Brussels sprouts, cut in half
½ cup toasted walnuts, coarsely chopped
A few thin slices of red onion
2 tablespoons pomegranate seeds
Chaat masala, for garnish
Cilantro leaves, for garnish
2 limes, cut into wedges

Make the Tandoori Masala: In a small skillet, on medium heat, add the cumin, coriander and fennel seeds. Stir occasionally for 3–4 minutes, until the spices smell toasted. Turn off the stove and let the spices cool completely.

In a blender on high speed, add the toasted seeds and all the remaining ingredients, and blend to a powder. You should have about ⅔ cup. Store in an airtight glass jar, in a cool place, for up to six months.

Make the Brussels sprouts: Preheat the oven to 400 degrees.

In a medium bowl, add the olive oil, Tandoori Masala and salt. Whisk to combine. Add Brussels sprouts and toss until well coated.

Lay the sprouts flat-side down on a baking sheet. Bake on the lowest rack of the oven for about 30–35 minutes, stirring halfway through. Check the bottoms of the sprouts to make sure they're brown and crisp.

Place in a serving bowl. Add the walnuts and lightly toss. Garnish with the red onion slices, pomegranate arils, a sprinkling of chaat masala and cilantro leaves. Serve with lime wedges.

Roasted Delicata Squash With Brown Butter & Calabrian Chiles

SERVES 2–4

Inspired by a cold-weather favorite at Pizzeria Delfina, Amisha Gurbani created this version at home. First, you brown butter and mix it with Calabrian chile paste, garlic and capers. That flavor-packed concoction bathes rings of delicata — one of the best winter squashes to cook at home, since you don't have to peel it. After some time in the oven, the squash is showered with cheesy sourdough breadcrumbs and hazelnuts for crunch. You'll want to make this one again and again.

- 1 medium or large delicata squash, cut into ¼-inch rings
- 4 tablespoons unsalted butter
- 1 tablespoon Calabrian chile paste, plus 2 teaspoons of oil from the jar for garnish
- 3 garlic cloves, minced
- 1 tablespoon capers, minced
- ½ teaspoon table salt
- ½ teaspoon black pepper
- 1 tablespoon olive oil
- ½ cup freshly ground sourdough breadcrumbs (from 2–3 slices)
- 1 heaping tablespoon Pecorino Romano, finely grated
- 1 teaspoon thyme, finely chopped, plus more for garnish
- 1 tablespoon hazelnuts, finely chopped

Make the squash: Preheat the oven to 400 degrees. Spread out the squash rings on a baking sheet.

In a small saucepan, on medium-low heat, add the butter. Keep a close eye on it: Once melted, do not touch the butter, and let it cook until it starts to brown, about 1½-2 minutes. Take the saucepan off the heat as soon as it turns dark brown.

Add the Calabrian chile paste, minced garlic, minced capers, salt and pepper. Stir until well combined. Pour the butter mixture over the squash rings and use your hands to evenly coat the squash. Spread out the rings so they don't overlap.

Place the sheet on the bottom rack of the oven and bake for 35–40 minutes, flipping the squash rings halfway through, until golden brown in color.

Meanwhile, make the topping: In a medium skillet, on medium heat, add the olive oil. After a minute, add the breadcrumbs and saute, stirring occasionally, for 3–4 minutes, until lightly golden brown. Add the Pecorino Romano and thyme, and mix to combine.

Place the roasted delicata squash on a platter. Garnish with the toasted breadcrumbs. Sprinkle the hazelnuts all over. Drizzle with Calabrian chile oil. Sprinkle more thyme on top. Serve immediately.

Roasted Sweet Potatoes With Yogurt, Curry Leaves & Nigella

SERVES 2–4

Curry leaves are one of those magical ingredients that adds a complex flavor that you can't quite place but must keep inhaling. Do seek out fresh ones — try Indian grocery stores and well-stocked markets like Berkeley Bowl. Swirled with butter and poured on top of sweet potatoes and creamy yogurt, they make this easy side from Nik Sharma feel special.

- 2 large sweet potatoes (about 14 ounces)
- ¼ cup unsalted butter, plus a little extra melted to brush the sweet potatoes
- Fine sea salt
- 12 curry leaves
- ½ cup plain Greek yogurt
- 1 garlic clove, peeled and grated
- 1 tablespoon nigella seeds
- ¼ cup thinly sliced scallions
- 1 serrano pepper, minced

Preheat the oven to 400 degrees.

Rinse and scrub the sweet potatoes under running water. Line a baking sheet or large roasting pan with foil. Cut the sweet potatoes in half lengthwise, place them on the baking sheet cut-side up, brush lightly with butter and season with a little salt. Cover the sweet potatoes with a layer of foil and tightly press the edges to form a tight seal. Bake until partially tender, about 20 minutes. Remove the foil and cook the sweet potatoes uncovered for an additional 20 minutes until the surface is golden brown, slightly caramelized, and a knife inserted through the center slides through with ease. Remove the sweet potatoes from the oven and let them cool for 5 minutes.

While the potatoes cool, melt the ¼ cup of butter in a small saucepan over medium heat. Add the curry leaves, cover the saucepan with a lid and let cook for about 1 minute, swirling the contents of the saucepan until the leaves turn translucent and crispy.

In a medium bowl, mix the yogurt with the garlic. Season with salt to taste. Spread the yogurt over a serving plate. Put the warm roasted sweet potatoes, cut-side up, on top of the yogurt. Pour the melted butter with the curry leaves all over the sweet potatoes.

Heat a small dry skillet or saucepan over medium heat. Add the nigella seeds and toast until fragrant, about 1 minute, then sprinkle them over the sweet potatoes. Sprinkle the scallions and serrano pepper on top. Serve immediately.

Kabocha, Mushroom & Kale Stoup

SERVES 6

Kabocha, a Japanese variety of winter squash you'll start seeing at farmers' markets in the fall, is ideal for soups, stews and curries because it absorbs liquid well. In this "stoup" — a cross between a soup and a stew — by Sarah Fritsche, it breaks down slightly, thickening the broth, but still retains its shape. (If you can't find kabocha, try butternut or acorn squash instead.) Flavored with miso and mushrooms, the dish becomes a hearty main with the addition of tofu. And if you use vegetable stock, it's vegan.

- 2 tablespoons olive oil
- 1 large red onion, roughly chopped
- 2 tablespoons minced ginger
- 1 tablespoon minced garlic
- ¼ cup red miso paste
- ¼ cup mirin
- 6 cups chicken or vegetable stock, plus more if needed
- 3½ pounds kabocha squash, peeled, seeded and cut into 1½-inch chunks
- 12 ounces mushrooms, stems removed and quartered
- 12 ounces tofu, cut into 1-inch pieces (optional)
- Salt and freshly ground black pepper to taste
- 1 bunch kale, ribs removed and roughly chopped

Heat up the olive oil in a large, heavy-bottomed pan over medium-high heat. Add the onion and cook until softened, about 4–5 minutes. Add the ginger and garlic and cook until fragrant. Stir in the miso paste, followed by the mirin. Stir to combine and let the mirin cook off slightly. Add the broth, followed by the squash, mushrooms and tofu, if using. Season with salt and pepper.

Bring the soup to a boil, then reduce the heat to medium and let cook until the squash is tender and just beginning to break down, about 35–40 minutes. If the "stoup" becomes too thick for your liking, add a little more broth to thin out. Add the kale and let cook until wilted, another 4–5 minutes. Taste and adjust seasoning, and serve.

Wine pairing tip: *This is a deeply earthy meal, dominated by the taste of mushroom and kabocha squash, accented by savory miso and tangy mirin. Seek out Gamay, which usually offers a beautiful mix of flower, fruit and herb notes. Gros Ventre, Tessier and Whitcraft all make California Gamays that are light enough to work well with this meatless dinner but still substantial in flavor.*

Clams, Caramelized Fennel & Sourdough Soup

SERVES 4

Picture a clam chowder bread bowl, warming you up on a foggy San Francisco day. While certainly fun, the tourist favorite doesn't really do justice to clams, which start tasting extra sweet come cooler fall weather. Christian Reynoso took the best part of the bread bowl experience — the sourdough — and stirred it into clam soup with caramelized fennel, another fall delight. He likes to shell some of the clams, making the soup somewhat easier to eat at the dinner table, but still keeping some shells for the visual drama.

- 3½ cups bite-size, torn sourdough bread chunks
- 1 cup dry, acidic white wine
- 1½ pounds clams, preferably small, such as Manila or littlenecks
- 3 tablespoons unsalted butter
- 2 medium fennel bulbs, sliced thin against the grain, fronds saved
- 5 garlic cloves, sliced thin
- 2 tablespoons chopped thyme leaves, divided
- 2 small bay leaves
- 1 teaspoon coarsely ground fennel seeds
- ½ teaspoon coarsely ground black pepper, plus more for serving
- ½ teaspoon red chile flakes
- Salt
- 2 cups chicken, vegetable or fish stock
- Lemon wedges, for serving
- Extra-virgin olive oil, for serving

Clean your clams by letting them soak in a bowl of cold water for at least 20 minutes and up to 1 hour. When you're ready to cook, lift up the clams to scrub them, placing clean clams in a separate bowl.

Meanwhile, turn your oven on to "warm" or to its lowest heat setting. Place the sourdough on a sheet pan and then in the oven to slightly dry out but not fully toast, about 20 minutes.

Set up a colander or strainer over a large bowl. In a large pot or Dutch oven, heat the wine over medium and, once simmering, add the clams. Shake the pot to settle them into the wine, cover with a lid and cook, lifting the lid once or twice to stir until the clams pop open, about 5 minutes. Turn off the heat and gently strain the clams from the cooking wine in the colander with a bowl underneath to catch the liquid.

Place the same pot back over medium-high heat and add the butter. Once it's bubbling, add the fennel and garlic. Cook, stirring occasionally, until golden in parts and tender, but not falling apart, about 7 minutes. You want the fennel to sizzle and caramelize while also not letting the garlic burn.

Stir in 1 tablespoon of the thyme, bay leaves, fennel seed, black pepper, chile flakes and salt to taste. Stir for a few minutes longer and then add the stock, reserved wine cooking liquid (which should be about 1½-2 cups) and 2 cups of water. Bring to a simmer, taste and season with more salt if needed. Turn off the heat.

At this point, shell all or half of the clams, or none at all.

Add the sourdough chunks to the pot, stir well to combine and soak most of the bread. Add the clams and stir again.

Immediately transfer the soup to serving bowls. Garnish with remaining 1 tablespoon thyme, more black pepper, fennel fronds, a squeeze of fresh lemon and a drizzle of olive oil.

Garlicky Eggplant & Potato Curry

SERVES 4–6

Most Indian food fans will know Baingan Bharta, the fire-roasted eggplant curry, but may not want to deal with charring and peeling eggplant at home. This eggplant curry, a vegan Gujarati dish shared by Amisha Gurbani, is far easier. You simply brown chunks in a pan, then stew them with potatoes and spices until soft. If you can't find baby eggplants, try Chinese or Japanese eggplants instead. As for the potatoes, any kind will work. Serve this with rice or naan for a complete meal.

- ½ cup vegetable oil, divided, plus 1 tablespoon
- 1 pound baby eggplants, cut into small chunks
- ⅔ pound potatoes, cut into small chunks
- 12 garlic cloves, cut in half lengthwise
- 1 teaspoon cumin seeds
- 1 teaspoon mustard seeds
- Pinch of asafoetida (optional)
- 2 teaspoons freshly grated ginger
- 1–2 green chiles, such as serrano, finely chopped
- 1½ cups finely chopped tomatoes
- 2 tablespoons tomato paste
- 1½ teaspoons ground cumin
- 1½ teaspoons ground coriander
- 1½ teaspoons garam masala
- 2 teaspoons Kashmiri red chile powder
- 2¼ teaspoons table salt
- 2½ cups water, divided
- 1 tablespoon brown sugar
- ⅓ cup roasted peanuts, finely ground
- ⅓ cup finely chopped cilantro, plus ¼ cup for garnish

In a large nonstick saucepan, on medium to medium-high heat, add ¼ cup vegetable oil. Once the oil is hot, add the eggplant chunks and saute, stirring occasionally, for 5–6 minutes. The pieces will be lightly browned on the outside. Remove eggplant with a slotted spoon, draining off any remaining oil, and set aside in a large bowl.

Add ¼ cup vegetable oil in the same saucepan. After a minute, add the potatoes and saute, stirring occasionally, for 7–8 minutes, until lightly browned on the outside. Remove potatoes with a slotted spoon, draining any remaining oil, and set aside in the same bowl with the eggplant.

In the oil left in the pan, saute garlic for 3–4 minutes, until lightly browned. Transfer to the bowl of eggplant.

Add the last tablespoon of oil to the pan. After 30 seconds, add the cumin seeds, mustard seeds and asafoetida, if using. Saute for 20 seconds. Add the ginger and green chiles. Saute for 20 seconds. Add the tomatoes and tomato paste. Saute for 30 seconds, then add all of the remaining dry spices and salt, and saute for 30–40 seconds, until paste-like.

Add 1 cup of water and stir to combine. Add the brown sugar and stir again. Add the sauteed eggplants, potatoes, garlic and the ground peanuts, and stir to combine well. Add the remaining 1½ cups of water.

Cover the saucepan and cook for about 12–15 minutes, stirring occasionally until the eggplant and potatoes are soft. Finally add the ⅓ cup cilantro and stir to combine. Garnish with more cilantro and serve immediately.

Lemony White Bean, Cheese & Chicory Quesadillas

SERVES 1

A quesadilla ... in the oven? Hear us out: Christian Reynoso's unconventional preparation is the lunch of work-from-home dreams, with a breezy cleanup and no need to babysit the stove. (Plus, the sheet pan makes it far easier to scale this recipe up and feed a crowd.) In this version, he fills the tortilla with creamy white beans, melty Oaxacan cheese and what looks like a full-blown salad. The chicories wilt down, adding a pleasant bitterness, and citrus enlivens the whole thing. Just try it, OK?

Olive oil
1 large (10-inch) or 2 smaller (6-inch) flour tortillas
3–4 ounces queso Oaxaca, mozzarella or Monterey Jack
½ cup cooked white beans (canned is fine), drained of their cooking liquid
1 large clove garlic, sliced thinly
1½ cups chopped frisée, radicchio or chicory greens of your choice, tightly packed
Flake salt
1 lemon, halved
Chile oil

Heat the oven to 350 degrees. Line a sheet pan with parchment, drizzle a little olive oil over (about 1 tablespoon) and use a brush to spread it evenly on the paper. Place the tortilla (or 2 tortillas, if using smaller ones) on top.

Tear the queso Oaxaca into thin strips. Arrange on top of the tortilla in an even layer. On one half of the tortilla, spoon the beans and sprinkle the garlic over them. Arrange the chicory greens over the beans and garlic. Sprinkle with flake salt, juice half of the lemon over the greens and drizzle with as much chile oil as you'd like.

Place the sheet pan in the oven and bake until the bottom is golden and crisp, the cheese has melted and the greens have wilted, about 8–12 minutes.

Fold the cheesy half of the tortilla over the half covered in greens and beans. Cut into smaller pieces (if you're making 2 smaller quesadillas, you don't need to cut them). Serve warm with a fresh squeeze of lemon from the remaining half of lemon.

Spicy Butternut Squash & Sausage Pasta

SERVES 4

This cozy, comforting pasta dish will swaddle you with its combination of caramelized squash and spicy fresh sausage inspired by chorizo. Christian Reynoso uses butternut squash here, but you could try a different orange-hued winter squash like acorn or honeynut. ("Winter squash" is a bit of a misnomer here, since they're harvested in the fall.) Avoid stringy spaghetti squash and drier kabocha.

- 4 tablespoons extra-virgin olive oil, divided
- 1 (2-pound) butternut squash, cut in half lengthwise and seeded
- Sea salt
- 1 ounce guajillo chiles (about 3 chiles), stemmed, deseeded and torn into small pieces
- 1 tablespoon tomato paste
- ½ teaspoon cumin seeds, freshly ground
- ¼ teaspoon freshly ground cinnamon
- ¼ teaspoon coriander seeds, freshly ground
- 1 teaspoon red chile flakes, freshly ground, or ½ teaspoon ground cayenne
- 10 ounces dried penne or other short pasta
- 8 ounces ground pork
- 1 medium yellow onion, roughly chopped
- 3 garlic cloves, roughly chopped
- 1½ teaspoons sherry vinegar
- 3 tablespoons fresh oregano leaves

Preheat the oven to 425 degrees. Line a sheet pan with foil or parchment paper and brush with 1 tablespoon olive oil. Season the squash flesh with ¼ teaspoon salt per half. Place cut-side down and brush the top skin with any excess oil on the sheet pan. Roast until tender and caramelized, about 45 minutes. Flip the squash and let cool. Scoop the squash into 1½-inch chunks onto the sheet pan.

While the squash roasts, add the chiles to a small pan over medium heat. Toast until fragrant, about 1 minute. Add enough water to just cover the chiles and bring to a simmer, turn off heat and let soak until softened. Once the chiles are soft, grind into a paste with 3–4 tablespoons of the soaking liquid, tomato paste and ground spices, using a mortar and pestle or a small food processor. Set aside.

Meanwhile, cook the pasta in salted, boiling water until al dente. Reserve 1 cup of pasta water before draining pasta and tossing with 1 tablespoon olive oil.

Heat a Dutch oven or the same pasta cooking pot over medium-low heat and add 1 tablespoon olive oil. Once hot, add the pork and cook, pounding with a wooden spoon until you have small crumbles that are just cooked through, about 5 minutes. Turn the heat down to medium and add the onion, garlic and 1¼ teaspoons salt. Cook, stirring often, until the onion softens, another 5 minutes. Stir the chile-spice paste into the pan. Cook until onion and garlic are very soft, and the color has darkened and thoroughly stained the pork and onion mixture, about 10–12 minutes. It should taste spicy and salty, but it will soon be tempered by the pasta and squash.

Stir the pasta and the sherry vinegar into the Dutch oven and stir well to coat. Add the squash and half the oregano. Stir gently to not break up the squash but disperse it well. Serve on plates with the remaining 1 tablespoon olive oil drizzled over the top followed by a sprinkling of the remaining oregano.

Wine pairing tip: *Caramelized squash, spicy sausage and toasted chiles make this pasta a good match for Cabernet Franc, an autumnal wine if there ever was one. Cab Franc tends to offer earthier, more herbal accents than its relative, Cabernet Sauvignon, and generally presents as a more delicate wine. The rich flavor of the chile paste-inflected pork should integrate well with a Cab Franc made in this piquant style, like those from Keenan, Lang & Reed and Florez.*

OPINEL
INOX

Peppered Short Ribs With Chicories & Caramelized Sweet Potatoes

SERVES 4

You'll need to procure flanken-style short ribs, also known as Korean short ribs, to make this cold-weather salad from Christian Reynoso. Many Asian grocery stores have them readily in stock. Otherwise, try seeing if your local butcher will cut to order. You'll season the ribs with gochugaru, the sweet-smoky Korean pepper flakes, and then quickly sear them. While this salad is substantial enough to be its own meal, sides of rice and kimchi would be welcome.

- 2½ teaspoons gochugaru, plus 1 teaspoon for garnish
- 1½ teaspoons freshly ground black pepper
- Diamond Crystal kosher salt
- 8 flanken-style short ribs, cut ½-inch thick (about 1½ pounds)
- 1¼ pounds sweet potatoes, cut into 1-inch wide wedges
- 2 tablespoons honey
- 3 tablespoons vegetable oil, divided
- 2 tablespoons rice vinegar
- 3 tablespoons fresh lemon juice
- ½ cup thinly sliced scallions
- 5 tablespoons extra-virgin olive oil
- 12 ounces chicory leaves such as escarole, Castelfranco or Treviso, torn or cut into 1½-inch pieces

Move an oven rack to the second-to-bottom position. Preheat the oven to 425 degrees. Line a sheet pan with foil and place it in the oven on that rack to preheat.

Mix together 2½ teaspoons gochugaru, the black pepper and 2 teaspoons of kosher salt in a small bowl. Using all the seasoning mix, season both sides of the ribs.

Place the sweet potato wedges in a large bowl. Heat a small pot over medium heat and add the honey, 2 tablespoons vegetable oil and 2 teaspoons kosher salt. Whisk until the salt has dissolved and the honey has melted into a thick slurry, about 3 minutes. Turn off the heat and use a spatula to scrape onto the sweet potatoes. Toss very well to coat.

With an oven mitt, carefully (it is hot!) take the prepared sheet pan out of the oven and place on your stovetop. Place the sweet potatoes on the pan so one of the cut sides is facing down, flush with the pan; set the bowl aside (you'll soon use it again). Return the pan to the same rack and roast the sweet potatoes until they are browned on the bottom, about 20 minutes. Using a thin metal spatula, transfer to a serving platter to cool. (If you let the sweet potatoes cool before transferring they may stick to the sheet pan.)

While the potatoes are roasting, prepare the salad and sear the short ribs. In the same large bowl you used for the potatoes, add the rice vinegar, lemon juice, scallions and 1 teaspoon kosher salt. Toss well and then add the olive oil and chicories. Toss everything together well. Add the still-warm sweet potatoes and toss again. Transfer the salad to the serving platter.

Heat a large skillet over high heat with the remaining 1 tablespoon vegetable oil. Once hot, sear the short ribs in batches so as not to overcrowd the pan, until browned on both sides, about 2 minutes per side. Transfer to the serving platter and continue cooking the rest of the ribs. Sprinkle the remaining gochugaru over the ribs and serve.

Wine pairing tip: *This recipe doesn't call for any outdoor grilling, but it's got the hallmarks of a great barbecue dish: smokiness, sweetness, spiciness and, of course, ribs. So open a bottle of Zinfandel, the ultimate barbecue wine. These flanken-style short ribs can handle a fuller-bodied, fruitier Zin (top examples include Limerick Lane, Carlisle and Ridge), but you could also opt for a more delicate version, like those from Nalle and Dashe.*

Miso Chicken & Rice

SERVES 4

Chicken, meet umami party. Jessica Battilana created this recipe after many, many readers begged her for more ways to cook their go-to bird. The flavors are big thanks to shiitake mushrooms and miso, and the technique can be used in other dishes: Chicken thighs start skin-side down in a cold, ungreased pan before the heat turns on. This renders the fat slowly, crisping the skin and causing less splatter.

2 pounds bone-in, skin-on chicken thighs, patted dry
Salt
3 tablespoons red or yellow miso, divided
10 shiitake mushrooms, thinly sliced
4 green onions, thinly sliced
2 tablespoons fresh ginger, minced or grated
2 garlic cloves, minced or grated
1½ cups sushi rice
1½ cups chicken stock
1 tablespoon unsalted butter, at room temperature

Preheat the oven to 350 degrees.

Season the chicken thighs on both sides with salt. In a measuring cup, whisk together 2 tablespoons of the miso with ½ cup hot water. Set aside.

In a cold, ovenproof, high-sided frying pan with a lid (or a Dutch oven) place the chicken thighs skin-side down in a single layer. Turn the heat to medium. Cook the thighs without turning or disturbing until they pull away from the pan easily and the skin is a deep nut brown, 8–10 minutes. Using tongs, turn each piece (if it's sticking and you're wrestling it from the pan, wait another minute and try again) and cook on the second side until browned, 3–4 minutes longer.

Transfer the chicken to a rimmed baking sheet and reduce the heat to medium-low. Add the mushrooms and cook, stirring often, until they're wilted and softened, about 3 minutes. Stir in the green onions, ginger and garlic and cook, stirring, 2 minutes more.

Add the rice and stir to coat. Pour in the chicken stock, then give the miso mixture a stir and add it to the pan. Increase the heat so the liquid is boiling, then turn off the heat. Set the chicken pieces on top of the rice, skin-side up, cover the pan and transfer to the oven. Bake until all of the liquid has been absorbed and the rice is tender, 25–30 minutes.

While the chicken cooks, combine the remaining tablespoon of miso with the butter in a small bowl and stir together until homogeneous.

Uncover the pan, remove the chicken and set back on the rimmed baking sheet, skin-side up. Preheat the broiler to high and arrange an oven rack 3 inches from the heating element. Smear some of the miso butter onto each piece of chicken. Transfer to the broiler and broil until the miso is sizzling and the chicken skin is crisp, about 2 minutes (watch carefully, because the miso can burn easily).

To serve, spoon some of the rice onto each plate and top with a chicken thigh.

Wine pairing tip: *Thanks to the miso butter and shiitake mushrooms, this dish packs a big umami punch. A skin-fermented white (aka orange) wine will be your friend here: Bottles like Jolie-Laide's Trousseau Gris, Matthiasson's Ribolla Gialla or Ryme's "His" Vermentino are all savory, copper-hued wines that become even more delicious alongside food with a little funk.*

Roasted Chicken With Apples & Mint

SERVES 4

When Nik Sharma roasts chicken, he likes to baste it in the oven with white wine that gets more and more flavorful as the meat cooks. For a taste of fall, he also tucks ground spiced walnuts underneath the skin and adds tart green apples to the pan. If you're heat-averse, skip the cayenne.

- ½ cup walnut halves
- 1 teaspoon garam masala
- 6 whole black peppercorns
- ½ teaspoon cayenne powder
- 1½ tablespoons Diamond Crystal kosher salt, divided
- 2 Granny Smith apples, cored and diced into ½-inch cubes
- 1 red onion, thinly sliced
- 2 lemons, halved, seeds removed
- 1 piece ginger root, about 1-inch long, peeled and cut into matchsticks
- 1 whole (3- to 4-pound) chicken, cut into 8 pieces
- 1 cup dry white wine or low-sodium chicken stock
- 2 tablespoons fresh mint leaves, torn

Preheat the oven to 375 degrees.

Grind the walnuts with the garam masala, black peppercorns, cayenne and 1 tablespoon of salt, to get a coarse powder. Set aside.

Place the apples, onion, lemons and ginger in a large roasting pan or baking dish. Season with remaining ½ tablespoon salt and toss. Set aside.

Dab the chicken pieces dry with a clean paper towel. Using your hands, gently ease the skin to create a loose space between the chicken's flesh and the skin. Apply the walnut seasoning in the space between the skin and the chicken flesh in as many places as possible, as well as on top of the skin. Arrange the chicken on top of the fruit and onions in the roasting pan. Carefully add the wine from the side and roast for a total of 1½ hours, or until the internal temperature reaches 165 degrees. After the first 30 minutes, ladle the liquids in the pan over the chicken every 15 minutes, until the chicken is cooked. (If you find the liquid levels dropping, just add a bit of water to the pan.)

When ready, remove the pan from the oven and cover loosely with aluminum foil for 30 minutes to rest. Garnish with mint and serve warm.

Wine pairing tip: *This recipe calls for a cup of white wine, so you might as well open something good. Look for a dry Riesling, which will play well off of the ginger, apple, lemon and walnut flavors in the dish and can withstand the chicken's spiciness. Some dependable Riesling producers from California include Tatomer, Desire Lines, Reeve and Trefethen.*

Gingery Bruleed Pumpkin Pie

SERVES 6–8

Did the world need another Thanksgiving pumpkin pie recipe? As it turns out, the answer is yes. Christian Reynoso's recipe ups the fun with a blowtorch, creating a glassy, crackly top like creme brulee. Use your favorite pie crust recipe or store-bought crust here.

2 cups canned pumpkin puree
3 eggs
9 tablespoons granulated sugar, divided
1½ cups heavy cream
½ teaspoon ground allspice
1 teaspoon cinnamon
2 tablespoons fresh ginger, finely grated
½ teaspoon salt
1 (9-inch) blind-baked pie crust, homemade or store-bought
Whipped cream, for serving

Preheat the oven to 325 degrees.

Mix the pumpkin puree, eggs, 6 tablespoons of the sugar, cream, allspice, cinnamon, ginger and salt in a large mixing bowl.

Place the blind-baked pie crust on the middle rack of the oven and use a measuring container with a pour spout to transfer the pumpkin mixture into the pie shell (this will avoid a scary situation like carrying a pie filled almost to the brim with liquid to the oven). Bake until the pumpkin custard has set but is still a little jiggly, about 1 hour to 1 hour and 15 minutes. Take the pie out and let it cool completely.

When ready to serve, sprinkle the remaining 3 tablespoons of sugar in an even layer over the filling. Turn your blowtorch on to low and position the flame away from the crust and over the sugar, about 6 inches away, moving around the sugared surface evenly until it's melted and golden brown to dark brown (a few darker spots are OK) all over. If at any point you see smoke and/or feel stressed, take a short break and come back to bruleeing the pie from a farther distance. Let the surface cool until hardened. Then carefully crack the surface and cut the pie into slices. Serve with whipped cream.

Cranberry-Orange Crostata

SERVES 6–8

A crostata is an Italian galette, a free-form dessert with a flaky crust that's far more forgiving than a traditional pie. Inspired by Thanksgiving cranberry sauce, Christian Reynoso fills this rustic version with fresh cranberries and chunks of whole orange macerated in sugar for a sweet, tangy, buttery finale.

- ½ medium orange, seeded and chopped finely (about ½ cup)
- ¾ cup plus 1½ teaspoons granulated sugar, plus more for the orange
- ¾ teaspoon Diamond Crystal kosher salt, divided
- 1½ cups all-purpose flour, plus more for rolling out dough
- 1 teaspoon ground cinnamon
- ¾ cup (1½ sticks) chilled unsalted butter, cut into ½-inch cubes
- 4½ tablespoons ice water
- 2 teaspoons cornstarch
- 12 ounces fresh cranberries
- 3 tablespoons heavy cream or 1 egg, beaten
- Demerara sugar
- Whipped cream, for serving (optional)

Toss the orange with ¾ cup sugar and ¼ teaspoon of the salt in a large bowl and set aside.

In the well of a food processor, add the flour, 1½ teaspoons granulated sugar, cinnamon and remaining ½ teaspoon salt. Pulse until well mixed. Add the butter cubes and pulse until they are incorporated and the size of pearls. Add the ice water 1 tablespoon at a time, pulsing after each addition, until all the water is added. Keep pulsing until the dough starts to come together yet still is slightly crumbly with obvious pieces of butter.

Lay a large piece of plastic wrap down on a work surface and transfer the dough to the middle of it. Use your hands to form a disc that's 1-inch thick and then wrap it tightly with more plastic (the dough might still be a little crumbly, but do your best to press it gently into a disc shape). Place in the refrigerator and chill for at least 30 minutes.

Meanwhile, stir the cornstarch into the sugar-macerated orange until dissolved. Stir in the cranberries and set aside.

Make sure you have an oven rack set in the middle of the oven, then heat to 400 degrees. Line a sheet pan with parchment paper and set aside.

Lightly flour a counter space you can roll the dough on. Take the dough out of the refrigerator, unwrap and place on the counter. Dust the top of the dough with flour (and as needed to prevent sticking) and starting in the center, roll into a roughly 14-inch circle — try rotating the dough after each roll to make a more even circular shape. Transfer to the lined sheet pan.

Transfer the cranberry-orange mixture to the center of the dough, leaving a 2- to 3-inch border. Fold up the sides over the edge of the cranberry-orange filling, pinching the dough as needed to create nice rustic edges. Brush the dough with the heavy cream (try not to let any excess drip on the parchment, because it will burn) or beaten egg. Sprinkle demerara sugar over the crust.

Place the crostata on the middle rack of the oven, turn the heat down to 375 degrees and bake, rotating halfway through until the cranberries have burst and the crust is golden, about 35–40 minutes. Let cool on a wire rack before slicing and serving with whipped cream, if desired.

WINTER

When asked what my favorite season is to bake in, people are often surprised when I say winter. At first it surprised me, too. Unarguably the plethora of fruits available in the summer is astonishing, but it's winter when I want to tuck into the kitchen and bake. It's more pleasant to avoid the cold, stay inside and shut off the world. Granted, living in Northern California in the winter is not like the Northeast where I grew up, but baking creates a warmth that is beyond physically warming the body. Winter is about nesting and allowing myself to slow down and focus on the moment — the feel of the tart dough as I gather it together in my hands, the stillness in stirring chocolate melting in a double boiler, the smell of a lemon pound cake when I open the oven door and stick a skewer in to see if it's done.

Luckily, living in California there is colorful produce in the winter months. When I walk through a farmers' market in winter, I cannot help but notice and be grateful for the assortment of Cara Cara oranges, Meyer lemons, tangerines, clementines, makrut lime leaves, finger limes, blood oranges, passion fruit, kumquats and pomegranates. These ingredients create bright, delicious desserts.

Even ingredients that are available year-round, such as chocolate and nuts, make different contributions come winter. They can be showcased more intensely — like in bittersweet chocolate souffles and walnut tortes — than in summer, when lightness is preferred.

I am like most people who bake in that I don't just bake because I want to eat it all. I want to share my desserts with my friends, family and, as a pastry chef, with complete strangers. A well-made dessert provides creative satisfaction, but there's also a joy in being able to share that dessert with others. This especially holds true with the winter holidays. Whether it is sitting around a table lingering over dessert and the last drops of wine with longtime friends, or leaving cookies on neighbors' doorsteps, desserts help us connect. Winter makes this all more possible, a time to succumb to the allure of the sweets of the season and all that they offer.

— EMILY LUCHETTI

Roasted Carrot, Bean & Goat Cheese Dip

MAKES 4–5 CUPS

Grab some heirlooms from the farmers' market for Amisha Gurbani's creamy dip, starring toasty spices, roasted carrots, white beans and tangy goat cheese. Once you take your hot carrots out of the oven, the recipe comes together as easily as whizzing ingredients in a food processor. The addition of whole carrots on top, dotted with pistachios, makes it feel like an elegant addition to a holiday party snack table. Serve it with cut vegetables and, Gurbani's favorite, ruffled potato chips.

- 1½ teaspoons whole cumin seed
- 1½ teaspoons whole coriander seed
- ¼ cup olive oil
- 1½ teaspoons table salt, plus ½ teaspoon
- 1 teaspoon black pepper
- 1½ teaspoons smoked paprika, plus ½ teaspoon and more for garnish
- 1 teaspoon sumac
- 2 pounds peeled carrots (regular or heirloom), halved and cut into 2-inch pieces
- 4–5 peeled heirloom carrots, left whole, ends trimmed
- 4–5 garlic cloves
- 3 tablespoons lemon juice
- 6 tablespoons extra-virgin olive oil, plus more for garnish
- ½ cup canned cannellini beans, drained
- ¼ cup goat cheese
- ¼ cup cilantro
- 2 tablespoons finely chopped mint, plus small whole leaves for garnish
- 2 tablespoons coarsely chopped pistachios

In a small skillet, over medium heat, add the cumin and coriander seeds. Toast, stirring occasionally for 3–4 minutes, until fragrant. Cool completely. Grind in a spice grinder or with a mortar and pestle.

In a small bowl, add the freshly ground spices, olive oil, 1½ teaspoons salt, pepper, 1½ teaspoons smoked paprika and sumac. Mix to combine.

Preheat the oven to 350 degrees. On a baking sheet, place the whole garlic cloves and cut carrots on half the tray. On the other half, place the whole heirloom carrots. Add the olive oil-spice mixture to the cut carrots and whole carrots and, using your hands, mix to coat well.

Place the baking sheet on the lowest rack of the oven, and cook for about 45–50 minutes. At the halfway mark, toss the carrots around to cook evenly. Remove from the oven and cool completely.

In a food processor, add the roasted cut carrots, roasted garlic, lemon juice, extra-virgin olive oil, beans, ½ teaspoon salt, ½ teaspoon smoked paprika, goat cheese, cilantro and mint. Pulse until pureed. Transfer the dip to a serving bowl. Spread and flatten with a rubber spatula. Garnish with a few tablespoons of extra-virgin olive oil and a sprinkling of smoked paprika.

Place the whole heirloom carrots on the top, garnish them with the pistachios and mint leaves.

Serve immediately with chips and fresh vegetables.

Note: *The dip can be made a couple of days in advance and stored in an airtight container in the fridge. Garnish just before serving. Store leftovers in the refrigerator for up to a week.*

Herb-Stuffed Baked Brie With Tangerine Jam

SERVES 6–8

Baked brie might feel retro, but Christian Reynoso's updated version will be the talk of any holiday party. Look for a relatively firm brie, so it's easier to slice the wheel in half before you stuff it with herbs. (If you end up with an extremely soft wheel, try chilling it in the freezer for 45 minutes first.) That herb stuffing melts into the rich, buttery dairy in the oven, and the flaky appetizer gets even more brightness from a side of freshly cooked-down tangerines.

8- to 12-ounce wheel of brie or Camembert
Flake salt and freshly ground black pepper
¼ cup chopped dill, plus more for serving, if desired
¼ cup chopped parsley, plus more for serving, if desired
All-purpose flour, for rolling out the pastry
1 sheet puff pastry, thawed according to package instructions
1 egg, lightly beaten
6–8 tangerines, such as Page
¼ cup sugar
3 sprigs fresh thyme
Crostini or fresh bread, for serving

Preheat the oven to 350 degrees. Line a sheet pan with parchment paper and set aside.

Slice the wheel of brie in half horizontally, creating two thinner wheels. Lay them cut-side up, then season generously with salt and pepper. Pile the herbs in an even layer on one seasoned wheel half and place the other seasoned half on top, sandwiching the herbs.

Lightly dust a surface with flour and place the pastry sheet on it. Dust the top of the pastry with flour then roll out into a square just big enough to be able to wrap over the cheese tightly. Place the herb-stuffed brie in the middle and fold the pastry edges so they overlap. Pinch all open seams tightly to make sure any drafty flaps are sealed. Place the stuffed brie on the parchment-lined sheet pan, folded seam-side down. Brush the pastry all over with the egg. With a paring knife or scissors, score the middle of the wrapped brie through the pastry about ½-inch deep and about 1-inch long. If you'd like, lightly score the top of the pastry (not into the cheese) with a design.

Bake until the pastry is golden brown and the cheese is threatening to bubble out of the top, about 15–20 minutes. Let cool for 15 minutes before serving.

Meanwhile, peel the tangerines and separate the fruit into individual segments, discarding any excess membrane. Set tangerines in a saucepan with the sugar, thyme and 1 tablespoon of water over medium-low heat. Stir to coat the segments with sugar and continue cooking, stirring often, until the tangerines are softened and jam-like and most of the bubbling liquid has reduced, about 20 minutes. Turn off the heat.

Serve the baked brie with the tangerine jam and crostini.

Wine pairing tip: *A rich, wintery appetizer like this one demands a refreshing aperitif: sparkling rosé. Bubbles will act as a nice foil for the toasty puff pastry, and the berry notes found in many rosés will play well with the herbs here. Most pink bubblies made in California have a little bit of sweetness — often imperceptible — to counter the wine's high acidity, which will work nicely with the tart tangerine jam you'll be making. Schramsberg, Ultraviolet and Roederer Estate all make excellent and affordable versions.*

Creamy Celery Root Soup

SERVES 6

Celery root might look intimidating, with its rough brown peel and patches of hair, but all it takes is the careful application of a paring knife to reveal the white center. The root is actually much more flavorful than the crisp green stalks, with a buttery, grassy aroma. Try it in Georgeanne Brennan's simple but satisfying French soup enriched with cream.

- 3 tablespoons unsalted butter
- 2 pounds celery root, peeled and cut into 1-inch cubes
- 3 stalks celery, including leaves, chopped
- 4 leeks, white parts only, chopped
- 1 shallot, peeled and chopped
- 1 teaspoon fine sea salt
- Pinch red pepper flakes or cayenne pepper, to taste
- ½ cup dry white wine
- 5 cups chicken stock or vegetable stock
- 1 cup heavy whipping cream
- Freshly cracked black pepper (optional)
- Chopped chives or chervil, for garnish (optional)
- Creme fraiche, for garnish (optional)

In a heavy-bottom stock pot, melt the butter over medium-high heat. Add the celery root, celery, leeks and shallot, and stir until the leeks and shallots are translucent, about 2 minutes.

Sprinkle with the salt and red pepper flakes. Add the white wine, bring to a boil, and cook, stirring and scraping the bottom of the pot, until most of the liquid has evaporated, about 5–7 minutes.

Add the chicken stock and reduce the heat to medium-low, cover and simmer until the celery root is tender to a fork, 15–20 minutes.

Puree until smooth with an immersion blender or in batches in a standard blender. Return to a clean pot, stir in the cream and simmer gently until the soup reaches a creamy consistency, about 5 minutes.

For an exceptionally smooth soup, strain through a chinois, return again to a clean pot, and gently reheat again to just a simmer.

Garnish with freshly cracked black pepper, chopped herbs and creme fraiche, if desired, and serve hot.

Spiced Tomato Soup With Horseradish Cream & Toast

SERVES 4

What's this? A tomato soup recipe in the winter? Christian Reynoso argues that preserved tomatoes are, in fact, a highly seasonal ingredient. In this case, whole, peeled canned tomatoes cook down into a simple, soothing soup, with no blending required. A savory whipped cream spiked with fresh horseradish makes it interesting. If you can't find fresh horseradish at a farmers' market, try stirring in a little prepared horseradish.

- 3 tablespoons unsalted butter
- 2 large shallots, sliced thinly
- 3 large garlic cloves, sliced thinly
- 1 teaspoon fennel seeds, coarsely ground
- ½ teaspoon coriander seeds, coarsely ground
- ½ teaspoon red chile flakes
- Salt
- Freshly ground black pepper
- 1 (28-ounce) can whole, peeled tomatoes
- 2 cups chicken or vegetable stock
- 1 teaspoon fresh thyme leaves
- ½ cup heavy cream
- 3 inches fresh horseradish, peeled
- 4 slices thick-cut bread, toasted

In a 3-quart pot, melt the butter over medium-low heat. Once melted, add the shallots, garlic, fennel seeds, coriander seeds, red chile flakes, ½ teaspoon salt and ½ teaspoon black pepper. Cook the shallots and garlic, stirring often with a wooden spoon (preferably a blunt-edged one) until they're very soft with some light golden edges, but no browning. As you stir, use the spoon to punch down on the shallots and garlic to break them into smaller pieces and so they cook faster.

Stir in the tomatoes and, with your spoon (or a masher), break up the tomatoes into small chunky pieces that would fit on a soup spoon. Pour in the chicken stock, turn the heat up to medium and bring to a simmer. Once simmering, turn off the heat and stir in the thyme. Season to taste with salt. Turn off the heat.

Meanwhile, as you're waiting for the soup to come to a simmer, pour the heavy cream into a bowl and whisk until you have soft peaks. Finely grate the horseradish over the whipped cream, stir until combined and then season with salt to taste. Set aside.

To serve, ladle the hot soup into bowls, spread the cream over the toasted bread and place the toast on top of the soup.

Leek & Roasted Mushroom Soup

SERVES 4

When rain falls, mushrooms say hello. Roast a mix of your favorite fungi for Christian Reynoso's soothing, vegetable-centric soup teeming with leeks, white wine and dollops of sour cream. Think of it as a heavy-on-flavor but light-on-the-body meal during a time of holiday overindulgence. Serve it with a hunk of crusty bread to soak up the broth.

1 pound mushrooms, such as a mix of crimini and maitake
3 tablespoons olive oil
2 tablespoons roughly chopped fresh thyme, divided
Diamond Crystal kosher salt and pepper
2 tablespoons unsalted butter
2 stalks celery, sliced thinly
6 garlic cloves, sliced thinly
2 wide strips of lemon or orange peel
1 small dried chile, such as cayenne or chile de arbol, crushed open
3 whole medium leeks, sliced thinly, rinsed and dried
½ cup white wine
5 cups chicken, turkey or vegetable broth
3 ounces arugula or chopped spinach
⅓ cup sour cream
1 tablespoon whole grain mustard

Preheat the oven to 425 degrees. Slice or tear the mushrooms into thin ¼- to ½-inch slices or pieces. On a sheet pan, toss them with the olive oil and 1 tablespoon of the thyme. Roast, tossing the mushrooms and rotating the pan once halfway through, until cooked through with some golden and crisp edges, about 15 minutes. Season with salt and pepper.

Meanwhile, melt the butter in a large pot or Dutch oven over medium heat. Once the butter is melted, add the celery, garlic, lemon strips, crushed chile and remaining 1 tablespoon of thyme. Saute, stirring with a spoon, until the garlic sizzles and the celery is soft but hasn't browned at all, about 5 minutes. Add the leeks and 2 teaspoons of salt. Cook, stirring often until the leeks have softened and melted down to about half their original volume, about 10 minutes.

Add the wine, turn the heat up to high and cook the leeks with the wine, stirring a couple more times. Then add the stock and bring to a simmer. Simmer until the leeks are very soft and silky, but still not falling apart, about 2–8 minutes. Turn off the heat, stir in the greens to just wilt. Taste the soup and season with salt and pepper.

To serve, mix the sour cream and mustard together with a fork. Ladle the hot soup into bowls, add a few dollops of mustard cream and then top with roasted mushrooms.

Savory, Sweet, Briny & Spicy Cauliflower Pasta

SERVES 2

Everyone loves a mostly pantry pasta recipe. This one is based on a dish once served at Zuni Cafe, where Christian Reynoso used to cook. He adds cauliflower for seasonality, sauteing slices with garlic, capers, raisins, anchovy for umami and red chile flakes for heat. After the prep work, the sauce comes together in about 10 minutes. Though scaled for two people, you can easily double it to serve four.

Salt
8 ounces spaghetti
4 tablespoons extra-virgin olive oil, divided
½ small red onion (about 3 ounces), sliced thinly
½ small cauliflower (about 10 ounces), sliced thinly
1 tablespoon unsalted butter
3 garlic cloves, finely chopped
2 anchovies, chopped
¼ cup chopped golden raisins
1 tablespoon capers, drained and roughly chopped
½ teaspoon red chile flakes
Chopped parsley, for serving
Finely grated Parmesan cheese, for serving

Bring a large pot of water to a boil, season generously with salt and cook the spaghetti until al dente. Reserve 1 cup of the pasta water and drain pasta.

Meanwhile, heat 2 tablespoons of the olive oil in a large skillet over medium-high heat. Once hot, sprinkle the onion over the hot oil. Don't stir or toss, just let it sizzle and caramelize until golden brown on the bottom, about 2 minutes. Add the cauliflower as well as a big pinch of salt and saute, tossing the cauliflower in with the onion until softened, about 3 minutes. Turn down the heat to medium-low and stir in the remaining 2 tablespoons of olive oil and butter.

Stir in the garlic, anchovies, raisins, capers and chile flakes. Once the garlic is aromatic, add the spaghetti and ½ cup of the reserved pasta water. Using tongs, toss the noodles with the sauteed cauliflower and onion. Keep tossing and you'll notice that as the pasta water heats up, it will thicken and create a sauce. For a looser sauce, keep adding more pasta water, ¼ cup at time, until you've reached your desired consistency. Turn off the heat and season with more salt, if desired.

When ready to serve, stir in the parsley, transfer to serving plates and top with the Parmesan cheese.

Kheema Pasta

SERVES 4

Nik Sharma's ideal comfort food? Kheema, the saucy ground meat dish — the first Indian meal he learned to cook with his mom. His version is full of spice and acid, thanks to a generous pour of apple cider vinegar. And while it could certainly be served with rice or bread, he discovered it made for an excellent pasta sauce in college.

1 tablespoon ghee or olive oil
1 teaspoon garam masala
½ teaspoon ground turmeric
½ teaspoon Kashmiri red chile powder
6–8 curry leaves
1 medium red onion, finely chopped
2 garlic cloves, minced
1 piece ginger root, about 1 inch, peeled and grated
1 medium red bell pepper, cored and finely chopped
1 pound ground lamb or ground beef
¼ cup apple cider vinegar
1 teaspoon fine sea salt, plus more for pasta water
½ teaspoon black pepper
2 cups mini farfalle
2 tablespoons chopped cilantro or flat-leaf parsley
2 generous tablespoons grated Parmesan

Heat the ghee in a medium skillet on medium-high heat. Once the ghee is hot, add all the spices: garam masala, turmeric, chile powder and curry leaves. Cook for 30–45 seconds, until the spices just start to release their perfume. Then add the onion and saute for 4–5 minutes, until it just starts to turn pink and translucent. Add the garlic and ginger and saute for 1 minute. Add the bell pepper and saute for 2 minutes. Fold in the ground lamb and cook for about 5–6 minutes, until the meat is well browned and completely cooked. Reduce the heat to low and add the vinegar, salt and pepper, and cook for 2–3 minutes, until most of the liquid has evaporated. Taste and adjust the seasoning if necessary. Remove from heat. Cover kheema sauce to keep warm.

Meanwhile, prepare the pasta. Bring a pot of salted water to boil. Add pasta and cook until al dente, according to package instructions. Drain and divide the pasta onto serving dishes. Top with the warm kheema and garnish with cilantro and cheese.

Spaghetti al Limone With Chiles & Dungeness Crab

SERVES 4

One of the simplest pantry pastas around, this lemony spaghetti gets its creaminess by emulsifying starchy pasta cooking water, butter and cheese. You could serve it just so, or follow Jessica Battilana's lead and throw in chiles and Dungeness crab. The result feels special and, frankly, much better than most crab pastas you'll find at restaurants.

Salt
12 ounces dry spaghetti
5 tablespoons unsalted butter
1 jalapeño chile, cut into rings
Zest and juice of 1 lemon
2 garlic cloves, minced
1 ounce Parmigiano Reggiano, finely grated on the small holes of a box grater
About 6 ounces picked crab meat (from one Dungeness crab)
Flake salt, for finishing

Bring a large pot of salted water to a boil and add the spaghetti.

When the spaghetti is approaching al dente, start the sauce: In a large frying pan over medium heat, melt the butter. When the butter stops foaming, add the jalapeño rings, lemon zest and garlic, and cook, stirring, until the garlic is fragrant but not brown, about 45 seconds. Remove from the heat.

When the pasta is al dente, use tongs to transfer it to the frying pan (or strain and reserve 1 cup of the pasta water). Return the pan to medium heat. Add the cheese and ½ cup of the pasta cooking water. With tongs, toss the pasta until the cheese has melted, the sauce is emulsified and looks creamy, and it coats the noodles. Add up to ½ cup additional pasta cooking water as needed. If the cheese begins to form a film on the bottom of the pan, reduce the heat.

Add the crab and some of the lemon juice, beginning with 1 tablespoon and adding more to taste. Transfer to serving plates, sprinkle with flake salt and serve right away.

Wine pairing tip: *This lemony, briny dish is the Platonic ideal of a Chardonnay pairing. The crab is the star here, so choose a Chardonnay that won't overpower it — one that leads more with citrus than with butter. A growing number of California wineries are making affordable Chardonnays in this leaner style, like Presqu'ile, BloodRoot, Olema and Chamisal. These wines should offer enough bright acidity to match the dish's zip of lemon, should refresh the palate after a bite of jalapeño and should let the crab's delicate flavors shine.*

One-Pot Brothy Pasta With Kale, White Beans & Sausage

SERVES 4

This warming bowl of pasta is just the thing for a gloomy day, when you don't have a plan for dinner and you definitely don't want to run to the grocery store. Jessica Battilana calls this a "back-pocket recipe, a dish you can throw together with things you have on hand that tastes greater than the sum of its parts." It's also extremely adaptable. Sub garbanzo beans or pintos for the white beans; grab whatever short pasta you have in the cabinet; use curly kale (or escarole) in place of lacinato. And if you're using store-bought chicken stock, opt for low-sodium variety, since the sausage and the Parmesan contribute plenty of seasoning.

8 ounces mini farfalle, rigatoni, casarecce or fusilli pasta
2 teaspoons olive oil
1 pound sweet or hot Italian sausage, casings removed
4 cups chicken stock
2 tablespoons minced garlic (about 5 big cloves)
1 small bunch lacinato (dinosaur) kale, stemmed and cut into ribbons (about 8 cups)
½ cup grated Parmigiano-Reggiano cheese, plus more for serving
1 Parmesan rind (optional)
1 (14-ounce) can cannellini beans, drained and rinsed

Fill a large, high-sided pot with water and bring to a boil. Generously salt the water, then add the pasta and cook for a few minutes less than directed on the package; it should be al dente. Drain, transfer to a bowl and toss with the olive oil.

Return the pan to medium heat, add the sausage and cook, breaking up the chunks with a wooden spoon, until still slightly pink, about 6 minutes. Pour in the chicken stock, scraping up any browned bits from the bottom of the pan, add the garlic and Parmesan rind, if using, and reduce the heat to medium-low. Stir in the kale (it will look like too much at first, but it will shrink) and cook, stirring occasionally, until the kale wilts. Stir in the Parmesan cheese and let the mixture simmer for 5 minutes. Stir in the beans and pasta, ladle into warmed bowls and top each serving with more grated Parmesan and a drizzle of chile oil, if using.

Note: *If you won't eat this in one sitting, it's best to add the pasta directly to individual serving bowls rather than the pot. Otherwise, the pasta will absorb all the broth.*

Gobi Manchurian

SERVES 4–6

Typically the cauliflower for this popular Indo-Chinese dish is fried to a crisp, then draped in a sweet-spicy-tangy sauce. But Amisha Gurbani devised a way to make a satisfying version at home with less mess, tossing florets in cornstarch and then baking them.

Cauliflower

Cooking spray
½ cup all-purpose flour
⅔ cup cornstarch, plus ¼ cup
1 teaspoon table salt
1 teaspoon Kashmiri red chile powder
⅔ cup water
1½ pounds cauliflower florets (from about 1 large cauliflower)

Sauce

⅓ cup soy sauce
2 tablespoons rice wine vinegar
2 tablespoons sambal oelek, Sriracha or any hot Asian chile sauce
1½ tablespoons brown sugar
3 tablespoons ketchup
1½ teaspoons Kashmiri red chile powder
½ cup water
1 tablespoon cornstarch
1 teaspoon black pepper
1 teaspoon table salt
3 tablespoons vegetable oil or other neutral oil
¾ cup finely chopped red onion
1 serrano chile, finely chopped
6 garlic cloves, grated
1 inch piece ginger, grated
2 green onions, finely chopped
1 cup finely chopped green bell pepper

Garnish

¼ cup finely chopped green onions
3 tablespoons coarsely chopped toasted cashews
1 tablespoon toasted sesame seeds

Bake the cauliflower: Preheat the oven to 425 degrees. Place parchment paper on a baking sheet. Spray it with cooking spray and set aside.

In a large bowl, add the all-purpose flour, ⅔ cup cornstarch, salt and Kashmiri red chile powder. Whisk to combine. Add water and whisk until viscous yet flowy in consistency. Add cauliflower florets to the batter and mix until all florets are well coated, then add the ¼ cup cornstarch and toss again to combine.

Place the florets on the baking sheet, doing your best to make sure they don't touch each other. Spray the florets with cooking spray. Bake for 20 minutes on the lower rack in the oven. Remove the pan and, using tongs, turn the florets over. Spray with cooking spray again. Bake for another 20 minutes, or until golden brown in color with some darker brown spots all over.

Prepare the sauce: While the florets are baking, make the sauce. In a medium bowl, combine soy sauce, rice wine vinegar, sambal, brown sugar, ketchup, Kashmiri red chile powder, water, cornstarch, pepper and salt. Whisk until well combined.

In a large skillet, over medium heat, add the vegetable oil. Once the oil is hot, after 2 minutes, add the red onions and saute for 3–4 minutes, or until translucent. Add the serrano, garlic, ginger and green onions, and saute for 30 seconds. Add the bell pepper and saute for 1–2 minutes. Add the sauce mixture to the pan and combine for 3–4 minutes, until slightly thick. Switch off the stove.

Add the florets to the sauce and toss well to combine, until all florets are nicely coated. Transfer the Gobi Manchurian to a serving plate. Garnish with the ¼ cup green onions, cashews and sesame seeds. Serve immediately.

Sole With Scallion-Miso Butter

SERVES 4

A winter favorite in the Bay Area, petrale sole is the king of sole — sweet, mild and rich, especially when pan-fried in clarified butter. Inspired by the French classic sole meunière, Jessica Battilana lightly dredges filets in flour before cooking them in butter and then saucing them in even more butter. In this case, it's scallion-miso compound butter. Even better: It all comes together in about 15 minutes.

4 tablespoons unsalted butter, softened
1½ tablespoons white miso
5 scallions, thinly sliced
1 pound boneless, skinless petrale sole filets (about 4–5 filets, depending on size)
Salt
½ cup all-purpose flour
4 tablespoons clarified butter or ghee (unsalted butter can be substituted)
Lemon wedges, for serving
Cilantro leaves, for serving (optional)

In a small bowl, stir together the softened butter, miso and scallions until well combined. Set aside.

Season each fish filet on both sides lightly with salt. Spread the flour out on a plate and lightly dredge each fish filet on both sides with flour, shaking off the excess. Transfer to a large plate or rimmed baking sheet.

In a large frying pan over medium-high heat, melt 2 tablespoons of the clarified butter. Add half of the fish filets and cook until golden brown on one side, about 2 minutes. Flip and cook until golden brown on the second side, about 1 minute longer. Transfer to a warmed platter. (If you are using regular butter, remove the pan from the heat and wipe it clean with a paper towel before adding the remaining butter and frying the remaining fish.) Add the remaining clarified butter to the pan and cook the remaining fish filets, removing them from the pan once cooked. Remove the pan from the heat and wipe clean with a paper towel.

Return the pan to medium-low heat and add the scallion-miso butter. When the butter melts and begins to sizzle, whisk in a few tablespoons of warm water until the sauce is glossy and smooth. Remove from the heat and immediately spoon the butter sauce over the fish. Squeeze a lemon over the top and garnish with cilantro leaves, if using. Serve immediately.

Cioppino, Your Way

SERVES 6–8

Can you have a San Francisco cookbook without a cioppino recipe? It's the city's original seafood stew, a favorite at old-school restaurants and a traditional holiday feast at home. There are also a lot of variations, so Tara Duggan created this customizable recipe. It's designed for mixing and matching, according to your personal preferences or what you have on hand. For each category, choose among the listed ingredients and add up to the total volume. (For shellfish, for example, you could use 3 pounds of crab plus 2 pounds clams and 1 pound shrimp.)

¼ cup fat (extra-virgin olive oil, butter)
¼-½ teaspoon spice (cayenne, red pepper flakes, chopped jalapeño pepper, black pepper, saffron threads soaked in warm water), plus more to taste
3 cups diced or minced aromatics (onion, leek, fennel, celery, green bell pepper)
2 garlic cloves, minced
2 tablespoons tomato paste
28-ounce can tomato product (whole canned tomatoes, diced tomatoes, crushed tomatoes, tomato sauce)
6 cups broth (clam juice diluted with water, fish stock)
1 cup wine (dry white wine, red wine)
2–4 tablespoons chopped fresh herbs, reserving some for garnish, or 1–2 teaspoons dried herbs (basil, oregano, parsley, thyme, bay leaves, fennel fronds)
Salt
6–7 pounds shellfish (cooked, cleaned and cracked crab; cleaned clams; cleaned mussels; bay scallops; peeled or unpeeled large shrimp; calamari, bodies sliced)
1 pound white fish (California sea bass, black cod, true cod, halibut), skinned and chopped into 1-inch chunks
Lemon wedges, for serving
Crusty bread, such as sourdough, for serving

In a Dutch oven or heavy-bottomed stockpot, heat the fat with the spice briefly, then add the aromatics, garlic and herbs. Lower to medium-low heat and saute, stirring often, until softened, about 12 minutes.

Add the tomato paste, and stir to dissolve. Add the tomato product and toss to coat in the aromatics. Simmer 3–5 minutes if using tomato sauce, or 15–20 minutes for other products, until the tomatoes lose their raw flavor.

Add the broth and wine. Bring to a simmer, then cook 15–20 minutes. If using whole or diced tomatoes, puree with an immersion blender until smooth. Season to taste with salt. (The recipe can be made to this point — the base — 1 day ahead and refrigerated.)

Return the cioppino base to a strong simmer, then add the shellfish and white fish in this order: clams (cooking time: 10–12 minutes total); crab (8 minutes total); mussels, shrimp, calamari, white fish (all 3–5 minutes total). Each time you add a new type of seafood, stir to submerge the seafood in the sauce, return the sauce to a lively simmer and then cover the pot.

Season with salt and spice, if needed, and garnish with the reserved fresh herbs. Serve hot with the lemon wedges and bread.

Wine pairing tip: *Seafood tends to want white wine, but cioppino's tomato base behaves well with high-acid red wines, too. A classic pairing would be Chianti, the famous red wine made in Tuscany from the Sangiovese grape, whose brightness, herb flavors and medium body make it a great match for this rich stew. California produces worthy wines from Sangiovese, too — especially wineries like Prima Materia, Stolpman and Ruth Lewandowski.*

Dungeness Crab Frites With Pickled Pepper Tartar

SERVES 2–4

If you ever tire of dunking sweet Dungeness into nothing but butter, follow Christian Reynoso's lead and make two sauces: a garlicky butter sauce with pickled peppers for roasting and a pickled pepper tartar for dipping. While you're messily cracking crab, you might as well eat fries with your hands, too. While you could make your own here, Reynoso suggests making life easier and grabbing a bag of frozen fries. Another perfectly acceptable shortcut: starting with cooked crab instead of buying a live one.

Crab

4 celery stalks
3 large carrots
1 large yellow onion
1 head of garlic, halved crosswise
3 dried bay leaves
2-inch chunk of Parmesan rind (optional)
Salt
2 live Dungeness crabs, 1½-2 pounds each

Pickled Pepper Tartar Sauce & Dressing

6 tablespoons mayonnaise
½ cup chopped parsley, divided
¼ cup chopped dill
5 tablespoons chopped slightly spicy pickled peppers, such as hot cherry or pepperoncini, divided
1 teaspoon lemon juice or white wine vinegar
1 tablespoon roughly chopped capers in brine, drained
3 garlic cloves, finely chopped, divided
1 teaspoon whole grain mustard
4 tablespoons (½ stick) unsalted butter, melted
Salt

Frites

1 pound frozen french fries
Salt and pepper

Fill a large pot with 5–6 quarts of water. Add the celery, carrots, onion, garlic, bay leaves and Parmesan rind, if using. Bring to a boil then season the water with enough salt to make it taste salty, but a little less so than the sea — about ¼ cup if using Diamond Crystal kosher salt.

Cook one crab at a time by grabbing the body with long tongs and gently submerging the crab into boiling broth. Cover with a lid and cook for about 12–15 minutes (about 7 minutes per pound of crab) then transfer to a colander and run under cold water; once cool to the touch, transfer to a cutting board. Repeat with the remaining crab.

Gently pull up the main crab shell exposing the main cavity, then scoop out everything that doesn't look like crab meat from the center and sides, including the feathery gray gills. Rinse again until clean. On the bottom of the crab, flip up the butt flap and tear off, then cut the crab in half, and cut the legs and claws into individual pieces. With a mallet or a nutcracker, gently break the shells open just enough to expose the cooked meat and set aside.

Preheat the oven to the temperature as directed on the french fry packaging (usually about 425 degrees). Position the two racks in the oven.

In a small bowl add the mayonnaise, ¼ cup parsley, dill, 2 tablespoons of the chopped pickled peppers, lemon juice, capers, about a third of the chopped garlic and the mustard. Mix well with a fork and set aside. In a small pot, melt the butter over low heat. Add the remaining garlic. Turn off the heat and set aside.

Bake the french fries as directed.

Meanwhile, in a large bowl, gently toss the crab parts, garlicky melted butter and the remaining 3 tablespoons chopped pickled peppers. Lay the crab parts on a sheet pan. Place the pan in the oven along with the fries and roast until the garlic is very aromatic, about 5–10 minutes.

To serve, sprinkle the remaining ¼ cup parsley on the crab and transfer to serving plates. Season the french fries with salt and pepper. Serve fries alongside the crab with the pickled pepper tartar sauce.

Soy-Marmalade Glazed Chicken Meatballs

SERVES 4

These Japanese-style chicken meatballs, known as tsukune, finish cooking in a wonderful four-ingredient glaze that Jessica Battilana learned from Rintaro chef Sylvan Mishima Brackett. It's an easy crowd-pleaser that Battilana swears even picky kids will happily eat. The most important detail is to obtain the correct soy sauce. You want usukuchi (light-colored) soy sauce, which is not the same as light (low-sodium) soy sauce.

Meatballs

1 pound ground chicken (preferably dark meat, though white meat or a mixture will work)
¼ cup panko bread crumbs
1 egg white
3 scallions, white and light green parts finely chopped, dark green tops reserved
1 tablespoon finely chopped fresh ginger
2 teaspoons sesame oil
1 garlic clove, minced
¼ teaspoon Diamond Crystal kosher salt
¼ teaspoon freshly ground pepper
1 tablespoon vegetable oil, plus more for oiling hands

Glaze

½ cup sake
¼ cup usukuchi soy sauce (see headnote)
⅓ cup orange marmalade
2 garlic cloves, minced
Toasted sesame seeds, for serving (optional)
Steamed rice, for serving

In a medium bowl, combine all of the meatball ingredients except the vegetable oil and mix well. With lightly oiled or moistened hands, roll the mixture into 16 meatballs and set on a rimmed baking sheet.

Heat the oil in a 10-inch nonstick skillet over medium-high heat. When the oil is hot, add the meatballs and cook, rolling them in the pan to preserve their round shape, until they're golden brown all over, 2–3 minutes (if they flatten a bit during the process, don't despair — they'll still taste great). Transfer the browned meatballs to a plate and return the pan to medium heat.

Add the sake, soy sauce, marmalade and garlic to the pan, and stir with a wooden spoon. When the mixture begins to bubble, return the meatballs to the pan and cook, turning them from time to time, until the glaze has thickened enough to coat the meatballs and the meatballs are cooked through (cut one to test), 10–13 minutes.

Transfer to a serving plate and top with some sesame seeds, if using. Thinly slice the reserved scallion tops on the diagonal and sprinkle over. Serve with rice.

Wine pairing tip: *These glistening, umami-packed meatballs can withstand a bigger wine than most chicken dishes thanks to the assertiveness of the glaze. Go for a Cabernet Sauvignon — preferably one that veers less toward bold, fruity flavors and more toward the spicy and black pepper notes that this powerful grape variety can produce. Di Costanzo, Maître de Chai and Outward each produce Cabernet Sauvignons that fit this profile; they're lighter in body than many contemporary California Cabs and extremely agreeable with food.*

Golden Chicken

SERVES 4

Jessica Battilana has been making a version of this creamy, yogurt-braised chicken for decades. It's inspired by a recipe in Julie Sahni's "Classic Indian Cooking," gradually adjusted over time.

- 2 pounds boneless, skinless chicken thighs
- Diamond Crystal kosher salt and freshly ground black pepper
- 5 tablespoons grapeseed or other neutral oil, divided
- 3 cups thinly sliced onions (about 2 medium)
- 1 tablespoon minced garlic (about 3 cloves)
- 1 tablespoon minced fresh ginger
- 1 tablespoon ground coriander
- 1½ teaspoons garam masala
- 1 teaspoon ground turmeric
- ½ teaspoon red pepper flakes
- 1¼ cups plain whole milk Greek yogurt
- ⅓ cup water, plus more as needed
- Cilantro leaves, for serving

Season the chicken on both sides with salt and pepper. Heat 3 tablespoons of oil in a large skillet over medium-high heat until shimmering but not smoking. Add the chicken pieces and fry for 4–5 minutes, until browned, then flip and cook an additional 2 minutes on the second side. Transfer to a rimmed plate.

Add the remaining 2 tablespoons oil to the pan, then add the onions, reduce the heat to medium and cook, stirring frequently, until the onions begin to brown, about 10 minutes. Add the garlic, ginger, coriander, garam masala, turmeric and red pepper and cook, stirring, for 1 minute. Remove the pan from the heat and stir in the yogurt, water and 1 teaspoon salt. If you have an immersion blender, you can blend the sauce directly in the pan until smooth. If not, transfer the mixture to a blender or food processor and blend or process until smooth, then return to the skillet.

Add the chicken and any accumulated juices back to the skillet, nestling the pieces into the yogurt sauce. Bring to a vigorous simmer then cover and cook over low heat, stirring occasionally, until the chicken is very tender and the sauce cloaks the meat, 25–30 minutes. Transfer the chicken to a serving platter. If the sauce looks greasy or separated, whisk in some warm water, 1 tablespoon at a time, until it comes together. Spoon the sauce over the chicken and sprinkle with cilantro.

Black Sesame-Chocolate Chip Cookies With Orange

MAKES 24

Holiday baking season usually means cookies, cookies and more cookies. Give the classic chocolate chip a twist with swirls of black sesame paste and orange zest, per Amisha Gurbani's recipe. You can make nutty black sesame paste at home with a food processor or swap in a store-bought version.

Black Sesame Paste

- ⅔ cup black sesame seeds, lightly toasted
- 3 tablespoons honey

Cookies

- 3½ cups all-purpose flour
- 2 teaspoons baking soda
- 1¼ teaspoons baking powder
- 1½ teaspoons table salt
- 1½ teaspoons freshly ground cardamom
- 2½ sticks unsalted butter, at room temperature
- 1 cup packed light brown sugar
- 1¼ cups granulated sugar
- 2 eggs, at room temperature
- Zest of 2 oranges
- 1 tablespoon vanilla extract
- 8 ounces bittersweet chocolate chunks or chips (about 70% cocoa content), plus more for garnishing
- 8 ounces semisweet chocolate chunks or chips (about 60% cocoa content), plus more for garnishing
- Flaky sea salt (optional)

Make the Black Sesame Paste: In a mini food processor, add the black sesame seeds and grind until a fine powder forms. The sesame seeds will start to release their oil. Add the honey and grind until you get a smooth paste with a thick, viscous consistency.

Make the cookies: In a medium bowl, combine all-purpose flour, baking soda, baking powder, salt and cardamom, and whisk to combine. Set aside.

In the bowl of a stand mixer, with a paddle attachment, add the butter, brown sugar and granulated sugar. Start the mixer on slow speed and gradually increase to maximum speed. Mix for about 2 minutes, until off-white and fluffy. Using a rubber spatula, scrape down the sides of the bowl and gather the mixture in the middle.

Add eggs one at a time, and mix to combine. Add orange zest and vanilla, and mix to combine. Then add the flour mixture in 2 parts, at slow speed so as not to splatter the flour everywhere. Mix until just combined.

Add the chocolate chunks or chocolate chips and mix to combine, so they are spread uniformly. Add spoonfuls of black sesame paste on different parts of the dough. Mix at a slow speed to just swirl the paste into the dough, about 5–10 seconds. Do not overmix, otherwise you will get a black dough. Place the bowl of dough into the fridge for about 30–40 minutes.

Preheat the oven to 350 degrees.

Line two baking sheets with parchment paper. Using a ¼-cup ice cream scooper or measuring cup, scoop out a ball and place on the parchment paper. Place up to 5 cookie dough balls on each cookie sheet, at least 3 inches apart.

Place sheets on the middle and lower rack of the oven. After 12 minutes, remove the baking pans. Bang each on the counter 2–3 times for the cookies to spread slightly and settle. Add about 3 chocolate chips on the top of each cookie. Place them back in the oven for 4 more minutes, for a total of 16 minutes.

If the cookies spread to odd shapes, you can use a spatula or a large round cookie cutter to nudge the edges into a round shape. Add a sprinkle of flaky sea salt, if using, on each cookie. Rest on the pan for 5 minutes and then place cookies on a wire rack to cool completely.

Repeat with the rest of the cookies.

Note: *The cookies can be stored in an airtight container for up to one week. Microwave for 10 seconds prior to eating for a fresh-from-the-oven experience.*

Kumquat-Strawberry Jam Shortcakes

MAKES 12

Emily Luchetti loves the combination of kumquats and strawberries, but their seasons don't exactly overlap. So she devised this dessert recipe using strawberry jam with poached, vanilla-scented kumquats and tangy creme fraiche. The biscuit-like shortcake dough is more forgiving than pie dough, but still take care not to overwork it, otherwise the results will be dense. You can poach the kumquats several days in advance and bake the shortcakes a few hours ahead, if you'd like, then assemble just before serving.

Poached kumquats

- 5 ounces kumquats
- ½ vanilla bean, halved lengthwise
- 2½ tablespoons honey
- ¾ cup plus 2 tablespoons sugar
- 1⅛ cups water

Shortcakes

- 2 cups all-purpose flour
- 1 teaspoon kosher salt
- 3 tablespoons sugar
- 2½ teaspoons baking powder
- 6 tablespoons cold unsalted butter
- 1 cup heavy cream, plus 1 tablespoon for brushing
- 1 tablespoon raw sugar or granulated sugar

Assembly

- 3 tablespoons soft unsalted butter
- ¾ cup strawberry jam
- 1 cup creme fraiche

Poach the kumquats: Cut the kumquats in half lengthwise, then cut each half crosswise. Pick out the seeds with the tip of a paring knife and discard them.

Scrape the seeds from the vanilla bean into a saucepan, then add the bean, honey, sugar and water. Bring to a boil over medium-high heat and boil for 1 minute. Add the kumquats, reduce heat to medium-low, and simmer until the kumquats are soft and translucent, about 20–25 minutes.

Remove from the heat and cool at room temperature. If made ahead, transfer to a container, cover and refrigerate; bring to room temperature before serving.

Make the shortcakes: Preheat the oven to 350 degrees. Line a baking sheet with parchment paper and set aside.

Whisk together the flour, salt, sugar and baking powder in a medium bowl. Cut the butter into ¼-inch pieces and add to the bowl. Use your hands to toss the butter into the flour, as if you were tossing a salad. Once the butter is covered with the flour mixture, press the butter between your thumb and index fingers to flatten it into smaller (about ⅛-inch) pieces.

Pour the 1 cup cream over the top of the mixture, then stir it in with a wooden spoon. When it is almost completely incorporated, turn the dough out onto a lightly floured countertop. Gently form it into a smooth ball and then pat it into a smooth disk 1-inch thick.

Use a floured 2-inch cutter to cut out as many circles as you can; place them on the prepared baking sheet. Recombine the dough, pat out and continue until you have 12 shortcakes. Brush the tops with the 1 tablespoon cream. Sprinkle the raw sugar on top.

Bake until golden brown, about 25 minutes. If made ahead, leave out at room temperature.

Assemble: Preheat the oven to 350 degrees. Slice the shortcakes horizontally in half. Place, cut side up, on a baking sheet, and spread them lightly with the soft butter. Reheat about 5 minutes.

Place the bottom half of each shortcake on an individual serving plate. Spoon about 1 tablespoon strawberry jam on top, then top with about 1 tablespoon creme fraiche. Spoon some of the kumquats and poaching liquid over and around each shortcake, then top with about ½ tablespoon creme fraiche. Top with the upper shortcake half. Serve immediately.

INDEX

NOTE: Page numbers in *italics* indicate a photograph of that dish.

A

B

C

D

E

F

G

H

I

J

K

L

Q

R

S

ACKNOWLEDGMENTS

Thank you to the San Francisco Chronicle's wonderful recipe columnists, past and present. We included recipes from Jessica Battilana, the author of "Repertoire: All the Recipes You Need" and a columnist from 2017 to 2022; Georgeanne Brennan, a prolific cookbook author whose Chronicle bylines date back to the 1980s; Amisha Gurbani, the author of "Mumbai Modern" and our "Modern Vegetarian" columnist since 2022; Emily Luchetti, the James Beard Award-winning pastry chef, author of multiple baking books and columnist from 2012 to 2014; Christian Reynoso, our "Bounty" columnist since 2020; and Nik Sharma, the author of "Veg-table" and "Season" and a columnist from 2016 to 2020. We also featured recipes from two former Food & Wine staffers, Tara Duggan and Sarah Fritsche, who have helped Chronicle readers cook many, many delicious meals.

Thank you to photographers Lauren Segal and Andrea D'Agosto for helping make these recipes come to life. We also featured photos from Andria Lo, Russell Yip and our cooking columnists.

We had a lot of help fine-tuning these recipes from Christian Reynoso as well as members of the San Francisco Chronicle Food & Wine team: senior editor Janelle Bitker, assistant editor Caleb Pershan, wine critic Esther Mobley, restaurant critic MacKenzie Chung Fegan, and reporters Elena Kadvany and Jess Lander. Thank you, also, to Esther Mobley for her expert wine pairing advice.

This book would not have been possible without the work of more Chronicle colleagues: editor for emerging products Sarah Feldberg, creative director Alex K. Fong, deputy director of visuals Emily Jan, multi-platform editors Barbara Jaramillo and Shoka, and designers Stephanie Zhu and Steven Boyle. Graphic artist John Blanchard created the illustrations.

Thank you to Chris Fenison and the entire team at Pediment Publishing for their help in making this book happen.

And finally, to our loyal readers, who constantly send us encouraging feedback and inspire us to stay in the kitchen. This book is for you!

 · ISBN: 978-1-63846-111-1

Published by Pediment Publishing, a division of The Pediment Group, Inc.

www.pediment.com · Printed in Canada.